Help and Advice From the Other Side:

Take advantage of the unseen resources around you

Help and Advice From the Other Side

Irene McGarvie

Ancient Wisdom Publishing
a division of Nixon-Carre Ltd., Toronto, ON

Copyright © 2012 by Irene McGarvie

Library and Archives Canada Cataloguing in Publication

McGarvie, Irene, 1957-
    Help and advice from the other side : take advantage of the unseen resources around you / Irene McGarvie.

ISBN 978-1-926826-00-4

    1. Spiritualism. 2. Self-realization. I. Title.

BF1275.S44M45 2011   158   C2011-900876-9

Published by:
Ancient Wisdom Publishing
A division of Nixon-Carre Ltd.
Toronto, Ontario, Canada

www.learnancientwisdom.com
www.nixon-carre.com

Distributed by Ingram

Disclaimer:
This publication is designed to provide accurate and authoritative information. It is sold with the understanding that the publishers are not engaged in rendering legal, medical or other professional advice. If medical or other expert assistance is required, the services of a competent professional should be sought. The information contained herein represents the experiences and opinions of the author, but the author is not responsible for the results of any action taken on the basis of information in this work, nor for any errors or omissions.

General Notice:
Any product names used in this book are for identification purposes only and may be registered trademarks, or trade names of their respective owners. The author, Irene McGarvie, and the publisher, Ancient Wisdom Publishing (a division of Nixon-Carre Ltd.) disclaim any and all rights in those marks.

Printed and bound in the USA

Contents

There Is No Death

1

As a Spiritualist, I "know" that the dead are still with us. My deceased loved ones have not ceased to exist, nor have they gone on to some heavenly existence beyond my reach, or to some eternal torment in hell. Unlike religions where we are told to have "faith," my knowledge comes from personal experience. But it is not necessary for you to "believe" that the dead are still around in order to use what you will learn in this book. Go ahead and think of me as delusional if you want, but, if you are interested, just try the techniques described in the following pages; pretend that you are actually talking to dead people, and you will be amazed at what you experience.

What is Spiritualism?

Basically, Spiritualism is a religion where the adherents believe that it is possible to contact the spirits of the deceased. In other words, we talk to dead people. We don't believe in a heaven or a hell, and we don't get any bonus points for converting people, so evangelism or missionary crusades are unheard of. Attend services regularly or sporadically; it's up to you. God isn't keeping track.

What do Spiritualists believe?

Spiritualists like to think of themselves as a pretty tolerant bunch who have no strict doctrines or creeds, but that is not exactly the case. Spiritualists do have a definite belief system but they prefer to call their beliefs "principles." There are numerous autonomous Spiritualist organizations around the world which all have their own version of Spiritualist principles but they are all more or less based on the Declaration of Principles of the National Spiritualist Association. I have paraphrased these principles as follows:

1. We believe in Infinite Intelligence. In other words, we believe in God, but not in the sense of an old man in the sky with a clipboard who keeps track of our good or bad deeds, more like a universal energy that connects us all.

2. We believe that the phenomenon of nature is the expression of Infinite Intelligence. In other words our God, or "Infinite Intelligence," is nature or natural law. These are the principles that control everything that takes place in the universe. We are all connected to each other through this Infinite Intelligence.

3. We affirm that a correct understanding of nature and living in accordance with natural law is our religion. In other words, we try to understand the laws of nature and live according to them. Our understanding of these laws is continually evolving as we learn more about how things work.

4. We affirm that the existence and personal identity of the individual continue after the change called death. This physical body will eventually wear out, but the real you, the person inside will simply step out of the body and continue on, like a graduation to a new life. The personality and the interests of the person continue on without a physical body. Does this mean that we don't miss having the person physically with us? Absolutely not! Knowing that we can still talk to them doesn't mean that we don't miss their physical presence in our lives. We still grieve like anyone else, but it is comforting to know that our loved ones are still around, and it is comforting to know that when we die the same thing will happen to us. What about reincarnation? There is no official position on reincarnation; some people believe in it, others don't. We have the freedom to study it and come to our own conclusions about it.

5. We affirm that communication with the so-called dead is a fact. This one is pretty self-explanatory: we know that we can talk to dead people and that they can talk back to us. Some of us are better at it than others, and sometimes it is easier than at other times, but it is a fact. Most people become Spiritualists after experiencing this first hand, when they have experienced something that absolutely knocked their socks off.

6. We believe that the highest morality is contained in the Golden Rule: "Do unto others as you would have them do unto you." In other words, be nice. Treat other people the way you would like to be treated if you were in their shoes. Are Spiritualists always successful applying this rule? Absolutely not. You only have to attend one Spiritualist church annual general meeting to figure that out, but most of us are trying. We understand that everything would work better if we just followed this one rule.

7. We affirm the moral responsibility of the individual, and that we make our own happiness or unhappiness as we obey or disobey nature's physical and spiritual laws. This is the principle that separates Spiritualism from most other religions. We believe in personal responsibility, that no one can take responsibility for you. You alone are responsible for your actions and the results of those actions in all areas of our lives. We create our own happiness or unhappiness (our own heaven or hell) in this life and after death as a result of our own actions. There is no one who can "save" us and there is also no Devil to blame for tempting us. Does that mean that we are free to do as we please, to indulge any of our evil desires? Nope, see principle #6 above. Besides, the law of cause and effect, or "Karma" as the Hindus call it, comes into effect. In other words, we believe that the things that we do will eventually come back to bite us on the butt. So feel free to do as you please, but remember that you will eventually reap the results of your actions.

Now principle #7 is where things can get fuzzy. There are some Spiritualist groups that call themselves "Christian Spiritualists." For some people the term "Christian Spiritualist" simply means that they admire the philosophical teachings of Jesus, which is basically just an extension of principle #6, regarding the Golden Rule. "Christian Spiritualists" often read from the Bible in their services. Unfortunately, so many people in the western world are so brainwashed by Christianity throughout their lives that as a result of this conditioning they try to combine Christianity with Spiritualism and you get a belief in being able to talk to dead people combined with some sort of notion of hell and the need for Jesus to die for our sins which absolutely violates the spirit of the principle of personal responsibility.

I attended a funeral at one of these types of "Christian Spiritualist" churches once where they actually had an altar call, (this is where the preacher laid on the whole fire and brimstone/going to hell business and asked everyone to come forward and accept Jesus as their personal savior). The whole thing made absolutely no sense to me in a Spiritualist church. Oh well, to each his own I suppose. I guess they are just trying to hedge their bets regarding the afterlife, and I should not be judging them for that, but I hate to see that kind of fear creeping into Spiritualism.

8. We affirm that the doorway to reformation is never closed against any soul, here or hereafter. There is no hell, no one is subjected to eternal damnation, and people continue to grow and learn from their mistakes throughout their physical life and beyond. Even someone who was the epitome of evil during their life can come to understand the results of their actions and evolve over time. It is not uncommon to have people in spirit make contact with people in the living to apologize for the things they did while alive.

The Fox Sisters and the Rise of the Modern Spiritualist Movement

While contact with the dead has been going on throughout history, the modern Spiritualist movement began during the 1840's in western New York State.

In March of 1848 two young sisters, Kate and Maggie Fox, began hearing strange knocking sounds in their home in Hydesville, New York (a small village halfway between Rochester and Syracuse). The neighbors were called in to witness the strange phenomena, and over the next few days the sisters developed a type of code that enabled them to communicate with the invisible source of the noise.

The girls were sent away to stay with family members in Rochester in an attempt to stop the spirit communication, but the strange rapping noises followed them.

The girls claimed that the noises were caused by the spirit of an itinerant peddler who was murdered in the house some time previously and was buried in the cellar. At the time the raps began in the 1840's, the neighbors dug around down there but didn't find anything. However, many years later, in 1904, the house was excavated and a skeleton was found, buried in the cellar wall.

The Quaker influence

A Quaker couple, Amy and Isaac Post, were friends of the Fox family in Rochester. After witnessing the "rappings," Amy and Isaac were convinced of the genuineness of the phenomena, and introduced the family to many of their Quaker friends. These people became the early core of Spiritualists. This association with the Quaker movement is how Spiritualism became involved in humanitarian causes such as the abolition of slavery and equal rights for women.

Celebrity mediums

The Fox sisters' fame spread rapidly and they became the first celebrity mediums.
Their older sister, Leah, became their manager and they were soon earning large amounts of money giving public demonstrations and private séances.

Horace Greeley, the prominent publisher of the New York Tribune became a kind of benefactor for the girls, which enabled them to move in higher social circles. Greeley was grieving over the death of his son at the time that he met them and so the possibility of contact with the dead was of great interest to him.

However, as their fame spread, the Fox sisters also attracted criticism. Some newspapers denounced them as frauds. Skeptics insisted that they were fakes who produced their phenomena in a variety of ways ranging from cracking their joints to some sort of hidden mechanical devices. Committees were created to test the powers of the sisters. Most tests simply involved posing questions to the spirits, but others were more ingenious. One test involved binding the girls tightly enough that they could not move, but the rapping sounds continued. A committee of women even stripped the girls naked in order to check the girl's undergarments to insure that there was nothing hidden that could produce the sounds. Despite all this, no trickery was ever proven.

The rise and fall of the early Spiritualist movement

The early séances were simply entertainment, but the religious implications of communication with the deceased soon became apparent and the religion of Spiritualism emerged.

During the 1800's, people were intimately acquainted with death. Today we try to insulate ourselves from death. Deep down we really hope that if we eat right and exercise that we will be able to live forever. Today most people die in hospital and death is seen as a failure of the medical system, while back in the 1800's most people died at home, were prepared for burial, and were laid out for visitation at home. Prior to the medical advances of the 20th century, the infant mortality rate was much higher than it is today. It is estimated that 30% of all infants died within their first year of life. So with death all around them, it is understandable how people in the mid 1800's were so attracted to the message of Spiritualism. The continuity of life, the knowledge that death is not the end, and that our loved ones are still with us, provided tremendous comfort and reassurance.

During the 30-year period from 1850 to 1880 Spiritualism became the fastest growing religion in North America and thousands of people would claim the ability to communicate with spirits. Unfortunately, the sudden interest in spirit communication attracted its share of frauds and con artists. By the late 1880's investigations of fraud began to increase and Spiritualism was on the decline with the general public.

Alcoholism

For the Fox sisters, money and fame took its toll, as both of the young women began to drink alcohol, and soon developed serious drinking problems, which eventually wreaked havoc on their health and mental states. By 1885, their personal lives were in shambles.

The two sisters had become a source of embarrassment to their sister Leah and other leading Spiritualists. Maggie Fox was called before a commission in New York to prove her mediumship skills, and, in her inebriated state, she was unable to perform. In early 1888 Kate Fox was arrested for public drunkenness and ended up losing custody of her sons.

The infamous confession

The two sisters were broke and had lost most of their influential Spiritualist friends. A newspaper offered Maggie $1,500 (the equivalent of more than $30,000 today) if she would confess that it had all been a hoax. The story was published in New York World on October 21, 1888, and she appeared publicly at the New York Academy of Music before an audience of more than 2000 people to confess. She denounced Spiritualism as a fraud and claimed that their sister Leah had forced them into performing as mediums for the money.

This was big news and was publicized extensively. Skeptics were thrilled, but most dedicated Spiritualists simply considered her "confession" the ravings of a mentally ill drunk.

Recanting the confession

Maggie Fox later recanted her "confession" in writing in November, 1889, but this news was not publicized with nearly as much fanfare as the original confession.

Within four years, both sisters had drunk themselves to death: Kate in July 1892 at the age of 56, and Maggie in March 1893 at the age of 59. They were penniless and were buried in pauper's graves.

How do I know that my loved ones are still with us?

So how is it that I can say with complete assurance that I "know" that my loved ones are still with me? I know this through personal experience. I have had so many experiences that have showed me that communication is possible and that my loved ones are still around and that they are aware of current events in my life. Unfortunately, a lot of the time the messages that people receive from mediums are so vague that they don't convince anyone but the most gullible. However, it doesn't have to be like that. A good message can provide real evidence.

In my case, my grandmother, my father's mother, was a medium. I grew up in Canada and she lived in Scotland; so my only contact with her was by letter or by telephone a few times a year, or during her visits to Canada, which took place every couple of years, or when I visited Scotland. I knew that she spoke to her "spirit guides" and she seemed to just "know" everything. I knew that she would really blow people away with the messages that she gave people, but I really didn't understand much about Spiritualism.

My parents did not really attend any church. I went to a Presbyterian Sunday school and to a Free Methodist summer camp, but that was more for social reasons than for religious ones. My grandmother was a very strong personality and frankly most people were a little intimidated by her. Her son - my father - was her oldest child and had absolutely no interest in Spiritualism.

My mother, on the other hand, was fascinated with the idea of spirit contact. She had lost most of her family when she was relatively young and she had gone to Spiritualist meetings and had readings with mediums back in Scotland; so together we dabbled in things like tea leaf reading and tarot cards. But as a young adult I became involved with the Pentecostal church, and I am embarrassed to admit that I really bought into all their doctrine, and gave up all involvement in the "occult." However, after a few years, I left the Pentecostal church and for a time was not interested in any form of religion.

So while I had always been fascinated by my grandmother's ability to speak to and relay messages from "the other side," I really didn't get involved in Spiritualism until many years later, after both of my parents and my grandmother had died. I was going through a particularly difficult time in my life, my husband and I were having

9

problems in our marriage and were close to separating, we were both at crossroads in our careers, we were struggling financially, and I just really wished that I could speak to my mother. Interestingly, the first message that I got, the message that changed everything for me did not even involve my mother. I have heard from her numerous times since then, but not that first night.

I knew of a Spiritualist church not too far from where we lived and one night on the spur of the moment my husband and I decided to go to their Wednesday night psychometry service. (I will go into more detail about psychometry later in this book.) We had never been to this church before, we knew no one, and like I said it was a spur of the moment decision to go and try it out. We sort of sneaked into the church and sat down, not really speaking to anyone. Someone stood up and explained that it was psychometry night and if we wanted a message we needed to put $5 in the offering plate and put some item of ours or a note into one of the randomly numbered envelopes next to the offering plate, and then we should just sit down and wait until the medium called out our number. We were told that even then we should just sit quietly and not let on that it was our number so that the medium would not know whom the message was for. Hmmm, it sounded interesting, so we each put something in an envelope and sat down to see what would happen. What happened changed my life. I know how corny that sounds, but I can't think of any other way to describe it.

The medium was an older Jamaican gentleman who was one of most amazing mediums I have ever seen, easily as good, or better, than any of the celebrity mediums that people flock to. I don't know his name, and for the $5 we placed in the offering plate it was obvious that he wasn't in it for the money. He picked up my envelope but did not open it; he just held it and began to speak. I will never forget what he said:

"Number 46. I've got a gentleman here, a father and

grandfather energy, he is showing me his legs, he says that before he passed he had sores on his legs from his knees down, and he wants you to know that they are all healed now, and he says to tell you that you are spending too much money."

The hairs stood up on the back of my neck. I had looked after my father for the last 8 months of his life, and among his other health problems he had huge massive sores on his lower legs that required daily dressing changes. So this was very specific. Even the comment that I was spending too much money, while probably true, was actually there to give me proof that it was really him. Growing up in a Scottish family, frugality was a virtue and throughout my entire life my father had continually told me I was wasting money, so that hadn't changed. Had the medium said something like "your father sends his love" I would have thought no, that doesn't sound like my dad, not that he didn't love me. I know he did, and he has come through many times since then to tell me that he loves me. However, for that first message it was more important for me to hear my dad the way he was in life.

As I sat there in shock the medium started to chuckle at what he was hearing from the spirit people who were talking to him and he continued on with his message:

"I've got your grandmother here, she's quite a character, it's hard for the others to get a word in, she's got quite an accent, she says to tell you that you are spending too much money, that you shouldn't even spend a bad penny, whatever that means."

All I could think was, "Oh my god they are really here."

The only time I have ever heard that expression "don't even spend a bad penny" was from my grandmother, and I can't tell you how many times people have described her as "quite a character." The stories about her are legendary. After her death my aunt paid for a bench outside the Cannongate Kirk on the Royal

Mile in Edinburgh as a memorial to my grandmother. Everyone struggled over what the dedication should say. What do you say about someone who was so, so, well, let's just say memorable. My aunt finally settled on "Elizabeth Hume McGarvie, unforgettable." So it was obvious to me, from the medium's reaction to what he was hearing from my grandmother in spirit, that he actually was speaking to her, and that she apparently hadn't mellowed much.

He went on to say a few more things that proved to me that both my father and my grandmother were aware of the things that were going on in my life and that basically everything would be fine.

Afterwards, I told one of my brothers what had happened, and his response was that the medium must have known I was coming and had done some research about me. Duh! No! I didn't even know that I was going until the last moment and where would anyone find out that kind of information about my family and me. It's not like we are famous, and besides, for $5 why would anyone even bother going to that kind of trouble? No, I can say with complete assurance that this medium knew absolutely nothing about my family or me when I walked into that church, and he wasn't reading my body language since it was an anonymous reading. I had not made any kind of response to his comments so he didn't even know to whom he was giving the message. No, I can say with complete confidence that this was a legitimate spirit contact.

The message that had been conveyed that night was exactly what I needed to hear to know without a doubt that the medium really was talking to my father and my grandmother. But you never know what constitutes proof for someone else. I remember being in a circle one time when a medium said that she had a message for one of the other students from her mother. The medium looked puzzled and said, "Your mother says to tell you 'grilled cheese sandwich.'" Suddenly the recipient of the message burst into tears.

The rest of us were confused. Grilled cheese sandwich? What was she talking about? It turns out that every time the mother and daughter had gone shopping they stopped at a restaurant for lunch, and every time the mother would order a grilled cheese sandwich. They used to joke about it, and now here was a medium telling the daughter that she had a message from her deceased mother, and the message was "grilled cheese sandwich." As far as the daughter was concerned, hearing the words "grilled cheese sandwich" was the best proof anyone could give.

So how did that psychometry service that night change my life? Well from that moment on I knew that death was not the end, and that my loved ones weren't suffering in eternal damnation in hell because they did not adhere to any particular Christian doctrine. All that Sunday school indoctrination and Pentecostal fear got flushed away - what a relief! But more than that, it convinced me that even after death our loved ones still care about us and want to be involved in our lives, which is the topic of this book. This experience made me want to learn more about Spiritualism. Since then the study of Spiritualism, and the unseen world around us, has become a very large part of my life.

Not all mediums are as dazzling as that first one

That night after the service was over we just sort of slid out of the church in shock. We never spoke to anyone on our way out, and I am sorry to say that I never spoke to the medium to tell him how accurate his message was. We went back a few other times but there were different mediums, but none of them even came close to that first one. We ended up finding another Spiritualist church where we eventually became members. I discovered that mediumship is something that everyone can do; it doesn't have to be a gift you are born with. I began studying mediumship and then eventually we discovered Lily Dale, which is a Spiritualist community in western New York State.

So why does the quality of mediumship vary so much?

Like I said, we soon discovered that the quality of mediumship varies tremendously. It can be dazzlingly accurate or it can be pathetically bad. If all you ever experienced was the pathetic messages, you would wonder how any intelligent person could ever fall for this. As a Spiritualist I find it so embarrassing when I attend a service somewhere where a medium gets up and says "I've got your granny here, she has grey hair, and is wearing an apron and making cookies in her kitchen, and she sends her love." Where is the evidence in that? Unless your grandmother was Mrs. Fields, I don't see anything there that would constitute proof. Another one of my pet peeves is when a medium gets up and says "I have a message from your spirit guide, he is a Native American named Tonto..." or "I have a message for you from the angel Gabriel..." Oh yeah? I'd like to see you prove that. If there is no proof, there is no real message, and it just makes us all look ridiculous.

Sometimes the mediumship is bad because the medium is having a bad day. It just isn't clicking. It happens to everyone. It is like you are seeing or hearing underwater, or through a thick curtain of fog. Who knows why? But sometimes the mediumship is bad because the medium has gotten lazy. No one wants to give poor messages, but sometimes it is easier to get up and spew out the granny with the cookies than it is to demand that the spirit people give us good messages with lots of evidence. Other times I think the fault lies with the spirit people. Some spirit people are just better communicators than others.

There are many reasons why mediumship doesn't always work as well as we would hope, and I will go into the reasons in more detail in chapter 8.

Reasons for the decline of Spiritualism

Spiritualism has so much to offer; it provides real comfort

to its adherents. So why is it not more popular? I think that Spiritualism has not recovered the popularity it had back at its peak in the 1880's for a number of reasons:

1) Poor quality mediumship.

2) So many cases of fraud throughout its history.

3) It doesn't sell fear.

This last item was pointed out to me by my son. I was moaning about why it is that you could shoot a cannon through most Spiritualist churches and not hit anyone unless food was being served, while ultra right wing evangelical Christian churches are bursting at the seams and building monster mega-churches to hold the crowds. It certainly isn't because the evangelical Christians don't have plenty of cases of fraud; they pop up in the news every day. My son pointed out to me that they draw the crowds out of fear: you just never know when Jesus is going to show up again and you don't want to miss the rapture and spend eternity in hell. Since Spiritualists don't believe in all that, why bother showing up at church unless there is a great speaker coming, food is being served, or there is a really good medium and you hope to get a message.

What happens in a Spiritualist church service?

Since most of us in the western world are products of Judeo-Christian religious traditions, Spiritualist church services tend to be pretty similar to other church services. Usually we open in prayer (some people pray to God, others use the term "Infinite Spirit"). We do some singing to "raise the vibration" (more about that later in the book). There is usually a time of hands-on healing. Healing is a big part of Spiritualism and it doesn't get as much publicity as the "talking to dead people" part. Well actually, the mediumship is also a form of healing as anyone who has experienced grief can attest, but the hands-on healing part of the service involves physical healing. We usually have a speaker who talks about something uplifting, something that we can use to make our lives better, and then finally the part that attracts most people initially, the message service or demonstration of mediumship.

In some churches the medium gives longer messages to two or three people in the audience, while in other churches the medium is expected to fire off short messages, more like greetings from spirit, to virtually everyone in the room.

The point of these public messages is not to tell you what to do, and no, they are not going to give you the winning lottery numbers. The point of the demonstration is to show everyone that those who have crossed over are still with us; it is the proof of the continuity of life.

Most people are drawn to Spiritualism after they experience grief

Most people discover Spiritualism after they lose a loved one and they find that their previous religious beliefs just don't provide much comfort. Every summer in Lily Dale, you see crowds and crowds of people desperately wandering the streets looking for a medium who can give them a message from a loved one. As the population demographics change, and the baby boomers are reaching the age when they are losing parents and other loved ones, the crowds are getting bigger.

Even the biggest skeptic would dearly love to get a really good message from a loved one. Who wouldn't give just about anything to have one last chance to talk to someone they loved? I know that my involvement in Spiritualism came from exactly that motivation. My current interest in mirror gazing and physical mediumship comes partly from the desire to spend time with my mother, to do more than just talk, to be able to go and sit and have a cup of tea with her, and have her give me a hug.

We are not at the mercy of mediums to get a message from the spirit world

The good news, and the whole point of this book, is that we are not dependent on someone else in order to make contact with people who have crossed over (the Spiritualist way of saying dead people). We can all learn to do it to some degree. There is no difference between you and any celebrity medium out there.

I love getting a message in church, or having a reading with a medium, so I am not suggesting that you shouldn't go to see a medium. All I am saying is that it is possible to connect directly, and the rest of this book will show you how.

"There is no death.
Only a change of worlds"

Chief Seattle

2

The Natural Laws of the Universe

What are the theories that mediumship is based on?

As Spiritualists we like to think of our beliefs as being scientifically proven facts, rather than simply theory. To be totally accurate not everything that we believe has been proven beyond a doubt. However, over the years, there are many things that have been proven.

There is no such thing as "supernatural"

One thing that is indisputable is that everything in the universe happens for a reason. Everything has a cause and an effect. Sometimes we don't really understand the natural law that caused something to happen, but that does not mean that there is not a natural explanation behind it. Phenomena that people sometimes refer to as "supernatural" are always the result of some natural cause.

The word "occult" simply means hidden or unknown; so to refer to something as an occult science does not imply anything magical or sinister. It simply means something that has not been clearly understood, or something that has been kept hidden from general understanding.

If we experience anything, it must have a natural cause. This includes not just things that can be perceived by our ordinary five senses, but also those that are perceptible only to the higher senses. Senses like clairvoyance and clairaudience are possessed by everyone, but lie dormant in most.

Everything vibrates

We now can prove what the ancient Hindus taught thousands of years ago: that everything in the universe is in constant motion. Even inanimate objects, which appear to the naked eye to be sitting still, are in fact vibrating. The difference between objects results mainly from the different rates of vibration. If we change the vibration of something, we change how the object appears to us. For example, the difference between ice, water, and steam is simply the result of the rate of vibration caused by heat. The difference between the color red and the color blue is simply the varying rate of the vibration of light.

We know that there are sounds too low and too high for the human ear to register, but which can be heard by other animals and can be measured by scientific instruments. There are also colors outside of our visible spectrum. Just because we can't normally see or hear something does not mean that it doesn't exist; it simply means that we are not attuned to or equipped to perceive it. So the idea behind developing your mediumship is to train yourself to perceive things that are outside of your normal range of perception.

There are unseen, interpenetrating worlds operating at different vibrations

Since our range of perception is so limited, there is no reason to doubt the possible existence of other planes of existence, just as real as the one we live on, but which are invisible to our ordinary human sight and senses. The apparent absence of these other planes of being is the result of the difference in the rates of vibration. Quantum physics suggests that entire worlds could exist in the same space occupied by us, but we are not aware of them because we are unable to sense their vibrations. Some vibrations are too rapid and some are too slow for us to notice.

A plane of existence is not a place, but a state, and so it is possible that two utterly different planes could co-exist in the same place and be entirely unknown to one another. There could be, right here and now, existing in the same time and space where we are, some planet which is invisible to us, with mountains, oceans, lakes, rivers, cities, and inhabitants which could pass right through us and our world. We are not aware of its existence simply because it vibrates at a different rate than we do.

It is difficult for many people to grasp this idea of different forms of existence, each having its own rate of vibration, occupying the same point of space at the same time. But think of it this way: at any particular point of time and space there can be numerous vibrations of heat, light, magnetism, electricity, x-rays, etc., each with its own rate of vibration, yet none interfering with the others. Similarly, every beam of sunlight contains many different colors, each with its own rate of vibration so that no particular one crowds out the others.

When we begin studying these concepts, our first impression is that each plane is one of a series of layers, which sit above and below. But once we understand that everything is made of up tiny points of light in motion, we then understand how it is possible for all of the layers to actually exist in the same place at the same time, interpenetrating each other without interfering.

Ghosts

When you understand this, you can see how it is that the place where you are presently sitting, reading this, could also contain numerous other beings or objects of which you are unaware and which do not interfere with your movement. Sometimes these different vibratory planes more or less overlap vibrationally and you get glimpses of another world, hence the experience of seeing a "ghost."

Who hasn't had the experience of "seeing" something out of the corner of your eye and then, when you turn to look, whatever it was is gone. You might have just been getting a glimpse of one of the other planes.

Just last summer I was sitting in my living room at the cottage, and a friend and I were talking when suddenly she said, "Wow, look at that." I turned my head toward where she was motioning and saw a semi-transparent man walk through my kitchen and disappear. My friend saw him in more detail, while I just saw the back of him disappearing into a streak of light. We knew that there was nothing for us to be worried about; we knew that there wasn't an intruder in the house. He didn't appear to be paying any attention to us at all, he was just going about his business when, for that brief period of time, our two planes intersected.

The ancient occult teachings have always proposed the presence of numerous planes of existence, of which our own particular plane is but one, and they have always said that communication between the various planes is possible under certain conditions. So how do we make it easier to connect with these other planes? One way is to change our level of vibration.

"Raising the vibration"

It is believed that we on the earth plane function at a lower vibratory level than those who have "crossed over." So, in order to facilitate communication between these two planes of existence, it is necessary for us to raise our vibration, and for those on the other side to lower theirs so that we can meet somewhere in the middle.

There are many ways to "raise the vibration" including:

- Music
- Laughter
- Enjoying nature
- Prayer
- Basically, being happy

Similarly, it is believed that there are lower vibrating planes as well, planes that we really do not generally want to communicate with. These are populated by unhappy, negative entities, and you can come into contact with these entities through negativity, depression, and fear.

The world of sensation

In order to understand how communication between the different planes of existence is possible, we need to understand how we sense things. A sensation is the awareness of an impression, made upon our mind through one of our sense organs. Our senses are the doors to the outside world. Most of us are not aware of how much we depend upon our senses for our understanding of that outside world. Think about how much your life would change if you lost even one of your senses.

We sense only vibrations

All of our five senses of touch, sight, hearing, taste, and smell are really just adaptations of the sense of touch. What I mean by this is that what we are sensing is the way each of these types of vibrations "feel" when they "touch" our sense organs. The vibration of light as it touches our eye, the vibration of sound as it touches our ears, the vibration of taste as it touches our tongue, and the vibration of smell as it touches our nose. All of these vibrations are relayed to the brain, which translates the vibration or sensation into what we think of as a "perception." Therefore our consciousness of the presence of something comes through our sense of touch.

Think of how our awareness of the world around us would be decreased if we lost even one of our senses. It is true that often in cases where people lose one sense the others seem to improve to compensate, but there is still always some limitation.

Correspondingly, you can imagine how if you were given one or more additional senses your perception of the world would be dramatically increased. Well, we all have additional senses and they are already present, but most of the time they are lying dormant, unused, just waiting for us to dust them off and put them to work. This is what we are attempting to do when we develop our mediumship.

Imagine the possibilities

Our senses show us only a portion of what is happening around us. Imagine if our sense of vision was able to feel electrical waves, x-ray waves, or magnetic waves. In that case we would be able to "see" things as far away as the waves of electricity could travel, and in the case of x-ray waves, (even though solid objects intervened) we could "see" things on the other side of the world. Theoretically, this could be possible if our optical nerves were more sensitive. Imagine what we could hear if our auditory senses were heightened, or smell if our olfactory senses were more acute.

If a new sense or two were added to our present senses, our perception of the world would change completely.

Synesthesia

Synesthesia is a condition where people experience the blending or crossover of two or more senses. For example, they might hear colors, see sounds, or taste shapes. No one is completely sure how it works yet, but scientists suspect that it might involve cross activation of the brain, where areas of the brain that are normally separate activate together.

The scientific community has been aware of this phenomenon since the time of the ancient Greeks. Sir Isaac Newton questioned whether music and color shared similar vibrational tones, and in 1880, Francis Galton (a cousin of Charles Darwin), published a paper about it. It has only been relatively recently that it has become an area of serious study. Drug use such as LSD and mescaline can produce similar effects, but it occurs naturally in some form in a surprisingly large percentage of the population. Estimates range from 1 person in 20 to 1 person in 200.

Scientists used to think that people with this condition were merely speaking metaphorically when they described a particular musical note as a color or that something tastes like a shape, the same as when we refer to a shirt as being "loud" or old cheese tasting "sharp," but it is more than just metaphor. For people who have this, it is like having an extra sense, and it opens up many possibilities. Imagine listening to music and seeing fireworks of color, or being able to understand complex mathematical formulas through color or shape. This is how many geniuses or savants perceive the world. Many famous historical figures are believed to have had some form of this gift or genius.

For those of us who do not come by this skill fully formed naturally, it is still possible to work on developing it to a certain degree. This is less crazy than it seems, since only a slight adjustment of our sense organs is necessary to experience this. It is similar to tuning in a radio station. It takes trial and error, and practice.

Vibrational attunement

Just like radio waves which can only be picked up by a radio tuned to the same frequency, vibrations from the spirit world can only be picked up by someone that is tuned to that frequency. You can only receive messages that emanate from beings with whom you are "in tune" - to all the rest you are deaf and unconscious. This is why it is so easy to get messages from some people in spirit but not from others. But, as I mentioned earlier when I talked about fluctuations in the quality of mediumship, even if you are able to tune in and receive the messages perfectly one time, the next time you attempt it, the connection might be terrible. This can be the result of a number of factors:

1) You might be having a bad day.

2) The spirit person on the other end is having a bad day.

3) Atmospheric conditions might be interfering with the transmission. Just like during a storm your television reception can go screwy, so can your mediumship. Personally I find rainy days work well; I don't know why - perhaps the water acts as a conductor.

Bad days happen to everyone. The only thing you can do is accept it, acknowledge that it just isn't working, analyze what went wrong, and try again another time. I suspect that much of the fraud that has occurred in Spiritualist circles throughout the last 150 years is the result of people (celebrity mediums) feeling so pressured to perform in spite of having a bad day that they come up with tricks to fudge it when it isn't working naturally.

Keep an open mind

As you read through the remainder of this book, don't be too quick to rule out something because you have never seen or experienced it. Just because you don't see something doesn't mean that it isn't there. It could just be that you are not presently in tune with that frequency. For example, I personally have never seen a fairy, so as far as I am concerned they are simply myths. However, I have seen and experienced some other pretty incredible things, and

I do know some very rational people who are adamant that they have seen and interacted with fairies and other elemental creatures. So, I am trying to remain open to the possibility, regardless of how silly it sounds to me at the present.

Also, I live in downtown Toronto, and I regularly see mentally ill homeless people walking down the street talking to and arguing with invisible companions. This always makes me wonder . . . could it be possible that they actually are seeing and hearing something real that I can't (or wouldn't want) to see and hear?

"I look upon death
to be as necessary to our constitution as sleep.
We shall rise refreshed in the morning."

Benjamin Franklin

3

The Power of Thought

Thoughts travel in waves

Thoughts are things - material substances that travel in waves - and they can travel along until they reach the mind of another person. The brain is like a human antenna. Even if we don't realize it, we are continually sending out and receiving thoughts. These thought-waves have the power of creating corresponding mental states in other persons with which they come in contact.

Thoughts and feelings are contagious

Everyone has noticed how different places seem to have different atmospheres. Some places just "feel" warm and welcoming and happy, while others create a feeling of suspicion and distrust. This is caused by the prevailing thought waves. Have you ever walked into someone's home and you just knew that the couple had been fighting; in spite of their welcoming smiles, you could just feel the tension in the air.

Remember your mother warning you about hanging out with the wrong crowd? Well, she was right. People are influenced by those around them, and it is not just their behavior that is influential; it is their unspoken thoughts as well. You see it in companies all the time. All it takes is one negative employee who infects the person next to them and before long they have turned the whole workplace into a toxic environment.

We see it in neighborhoods too. Wealthy neighborhoods usually give off a feeling of confidence and possibility, while poor neighborhoods vibrate with negativity and lack, reflecting the thoughts and feelings of the inhabitants. Inhabitants of entire cities or countries can become influenced by the thoughts of one strong willed person.

Wars are caused or prevented by our prevailing thoughts. Great waves of feeling such as political enthusiasm, or prejudice for or against certain people, or groups of people, sweep over places and cause people to act in a manner that they often regret afterward when they consider the matter in the light of cold reason.

So why is it that we are not constantly swept off of our feet by these great waves of mental vibrations? Partly because many conflicting mental currents neutralize each other, and thus cease to exert any marked effect, and partly because many people are "immune" to the thought waves reaching them.

To understand this, visualize a busy metropolitan street corner. As you stand there, you are assaulted by a multitude of sights and sounds (anyone who lives in a big city knows what I am talking about) - but we hear few of these, and see even fewer. The rest of these impressions are lost to us. We hear and see only those impressions that are strong enough to catch our attention.

Most of the time, we float along totally oblivious to what is going on around us. In the same way we fail to perceive the numerous thought vibrations and mental currents constantly surrounding us, and we fail to notice the spirit activity that is constantly surrounding us. Generally we have to consciously make an effort to notice what is going on around us for us to be fully aware of it.

Mental attunement

We more readily receive and accept those thought vibrations that are in harmony with our own habitual mental states; and we tend to fail to notice those vibrations that are inharmonious to us for the same reason.

Have you ever noticed how right after you buy a new car, like a blue Toyota Matrix, suddenly the roads are filled with blue Toyotas. Is this because Toyota had a sale on blue cars? No, it is just because now you are suddenly noticing them.

So, what do you find yourself noticing on a daily basis? Whether it is positive or negative, this is what you are attuned to.

Once you understand the effect of thought waves you are better able to avoid falling victim to undesirable thoughts. We realize that we do not have to be open to the influence of every stray thought or feeling that happens to be floating around in our general vicinity. We can insulate ourselves from undesirable mental influences and attract desirable influences to ourselves.

Residual energy

There are some places that are filled with the thought vibrations of minds that have long since passed out of the body. Often these are places filled with the strong vibrations of tragedies that took place there. Gettysburg is one example of this, and the battlefield of Culloden in Scotland is another similar example. No sensitive person can visit these places without feeling some of the pain.

Even if nothing particularly painful or dramatic took place there, every place has some residual energy of its own which has an effect upon persons moving into it. Some places feel lively, some dull, some happy, some depressing. This is the result of the thought waves left behind by previous residents. Persons moving into these places are affected by the residual energy there, either positively or negatively. However, if one is mentally strong enough, they can help to change the mental tone of the place.

Voluntary and involuntary thought transmissions

Thought vibrations can be transmitted voluntarily or involuntarily. Involuntary thought vibrations are thought waves that are sent out unintentionally without any clearly defined intent to accomplish anything. Voluntary thought transmissions are those that are charged with strong desire focused to a definite point by clear-cut goals or intentions. This is commonly known as "telepathy."

Usually senders are unaware that their thought waves have any actual effect upon the minds of other people, but once you understand that thought is an active power, you can deliberately choose to send forth thought waves directed toward the person or persons you wish to affect and influence.

White "magic," or the positive use of mind power

I hate to use the word "magic" because it sounds like I am describing something supernatural, and, as I pointed out earlier; there is no such thing as supernatural. Everything that happens is natural and is the result of cause and effect. What I am referring to when I use the expression "white magic" is voluntary mental influence with the intention of producing results beneficial to the person being influenced. For example, anyone familiar with Florence Scovel-Shinn's writings (*"The Game of Life and How to Play It,"* etc.) is familiar with the expression "treating." She refers to people being "treated" for Health, Happiness, and Prosperity. She talks of speaking the word for someone's benefit. In such cases, the person influenced willingly opens up to the helpful thought of the person doing the "treating," and thus a co-operation and mental "team work" takes place with beneficial results.

So this category of "white magic" consists of all those efforts of mental healing, and similar metaphysical therapeutics directed toward the general happiness and welfare of the person being "treated." It generally takes place with the "treated" person's consent.

Amongst Spiritualists, it is very common when someone is ill or injured for other people to say that they "see" the person healthy and well. This is because of this understanding of how powerful thoughts and words are. You can see how important it is to think of things the way you want them to be, rather than worrying or visualizing negative outcomes.

Black "magic," or the negative use of mind power

There are always two poles to everything in nature. Whenever we find a force or power producing beneficial results, we find that the same force or power, turned in another direction, or possibly reversed in its action, will produce results of an opposite character. In this case "black magic" refers to efforts that produce results beneficial to the person exerting the influence, which is often to the detriment of the person being influenced. In other words, it is the use of psychic force for selfish and unworthy ends.

Once you become aware of the power of your mind there is the temptation to use it to manipulate other people. This is a very dangerous practice. As I mentioned earlier, everything we do to other people will eventually come back on us, so think very long and hard before you attempt any sort of manipulation. That includes something that you think is in the best interest of the person you are attempting to manipulate. Often what we think is in someone's best interest is not what he or she wants, nor does it turn out to be in his or her best interests at all.

Basically, both white and black magic work the same way. You fix an image (a thought) in your mind regarding the thing you want to have happen, you hold a concentrated mental picture there, and send out thought waves toward the person or the thing that you desire to affect. Imagine it as if it has happened, and feel the emotion as though it had already taken place. This, in a nutshell, is the visualization process described in *"The Secret."* It works, and, once you master it, you will be amazed at what you can accomplish with this technique. However, think it through very carefully before you do it for, or to, anyone without their express consent.

How can you tell if someone is attempting to use their thoughts to coerce you in some way? Well, basically, if you feel yourself inclined toward doing something that in your heart you know is not in your best interest, it is possible that someone else is putting the idea into your mind in this way.

How can I protect myself?

The best way to protect yourself from influence from outside sources is to be consciously aware of your own thoughts and have conscious goals and objectives. People who are at the greatest risk of undue influence from others are those who just float along with the herd, going whichever way the wind blows. Our governments, the media, and advertisers all take advantage of people who choose not to think for themselves.

Personally, I am never afraid of any sort of psychic attacks because I know that I attract to myself only things that are in harmony with my own thoughts and desires. This is also why I never fear making contact with the spirit world. I know that the only entities I ever run across are those that I am in harmony with.

So rather than worry about the goals and motivations of

others, either on this plane or any other, I know that it is far more important to carefully analyze my own goals and motivations to ensure that they are always for the highest and best.

Also, simply refuse to allow anyone to manipulate you. By consciously denying that anyone has any power over you, you neutralize the psychic power of such a person, at least so far as its effect upon yourself is concerned. The average person, not knowing this, is far more susceptible to the psychic influences of other people.

When you have this sort of positive mental attitude you will find that negative or manipulative people will be repelled by you and will either stop attempting to control you or else will simply disappear from your life.

The power of fear

It is important to refuse to admit to your mind any feeling of fear regarding the influence of other persons, for such fear opens the door to influence. You must take the mental position that you are absolutely immune to psychic attack or influence.

Voodoo practitioners are literally able to scare their victims to death. The secret is that their victims believe in and fear the voodoo power. The greater the belief in and fear of the power of some other person, the greater the susceptibility to their influence.

I visited the war museum in Yper, Belgium, a few years ago where I saw a wonderful exhibit showing how governments throughout history have used the media to manipulate the general public by instilling fear. By instilling unwarranted fear they are able to get us to agree to things that we would never normally agree to. One of the most successful techniques is through the use of visual imagery.

The power of visual imagery

A voodoo practitioner moulds little figures of clay, or of wax, in the general shape and appearance of the person they wish to affect. The superstitious believe that these little figures are endowed with some supernatural powers, but in reality the whole power of the little figures comes from the fact that they aid the imagination of the spell-worker in forming a mental image of the person they want to influence. This establishes a strong mental rapport.

The technique of using visual imagery itself is neither good nor evil. Churchill inspired the British people to defend their small island nation during WW2 by creating word pictures in his radio speeches. Hitler manipulated the German people through the visual imagery of his huge rallies and newsreels that his propaganda ministry created. More recently, the world was manipulated into invading Afghanistan and Iraq through the continually repeated images of the World Trade Towers coming down after September 11.

We can use this same technique for our own benefit by creating "vision boards," which are pictures of things that we want to manifest in our own lives. It is exactly the same principle.

Telepathy

In a sense, all forms of thought transmission could be considered forms of telepathy, but we generally think of telepathy as conscious thought transference in which there is, in effect, an agreement between the telepathic sender and the telepathic receiver.

This agreement doesn't have to be a conscious one; the agreement can be more tacit in nature. Telepathy takes place naturally when two people have established a close rapport. There are numerous documented cases of twins who know what the other one is thinking or experiencing even if they are miles apart.

Husbands and wives often finish each other's sentences, and who hasn't had the experience of thinking of a friend only to have the telephone ring a moment later and the friend is on the phone? These are all examples of telepathy.

Contact with those in the spirit world takes place through telepathy as well. You are hearing them in you mind, not in your physical ears. You are talking to them in your head; you are seeing them in your mind. The closer a connection or friendship you have with the person on the other side that is your contact (your spirit guide), the easier it becomes to make the connection.

Anyone can develop a certain degree of telepathy: sending, receiving, or both, through practice. Generally it involves cultivating your ability to concentrate, and this is best done through meditation, which we will discuss later in this book.

Is it just your imagination?

The big issue for most people is the ability to recognize when they are receiving something and trusting that you have actually received something versus "making it up." This is a problem because so much of it feels like you are making it up in your mind, like you are talking to yourself.

This struck me vividly during one of the first "development" classes I attended. I was sitting in a circle among a large group of people that I didn't know. We began by introducing ourselves, just saying our first names, then the leader put on some meditation music and we all sat quietly waiting to see if we "got" anything.

I really didn't have a clue what to do or what to expect so I just relaxed and enjoyed the music and tried to clear my mind. I got a very vague fuzzy impression of a Victorian era row house of the sort that are very common in downtown Toronto and I remember saying to myself, "Oh, a Victorian house." Thinking that this was just my mind wandering I went back to trying to meditate and clearing my mind. Next I got an impression of a woman in a high-necked Victorian style blouse with her hair pulled back in a bun. It still felt like I was just failing miserably at clearing my mind, but I decided to play with what I was seeing, so mentally I said to the woman "Who are you?"

She replied, pointing to a woman on the other side of the room (keep in mind that my eyes were closed during all this so I can't explain exactly how she pointed to someone, but I got the very distinct impression of where she was pointing), "I'm her spinster great aunt."

I remember thinking that this was an odd way of saying it. I couldn't remember ever using the word "spinster" to describe someone, but it still just felt like I was making it all up. So I just went with it and asked her what her name was. She told me her name was Clara.

Now while everyone in the development group was introducing themselves at the beginning of the circle, one of the women had introduced herself as Clara, so I assumed that I had just pulled up a name that I had recently heard, so I said to the "imaginary" woman in my mind, "Oh come on, if I'm just making this up, surely I can come up with a more original name than that."

The voice in my head replied, "Well actually it is Clarissa, but everyone knew mc as Clara."

She went on to tell me that there was a picture of her in her great niece's house and that the house she had lived in was very similar to her niece's, but obviously missing the modern conveniences. We had a pleasant conversation, but the whole thing felt like I was talking to myself, just making it up.

Then the group leader turned off the music and we each took turns saying what we had "gotten." When it got to my turn I felt a little foolish but I pointed to the woman on the other side of the room and said, "I was talking to a woman who said she was your spinster great aunt, and that she lived in a Victorian house similar to the one you live in."

She replied, "Yes, I do live in a Victorian house, and that would be my grandmother's sister you were talking to."

Wow, confirmation! So I went on, "She said her name was Clarissa."

The woman across the room from me frowned thoughtfully and said, "Well I suppose her real name might have been Clarissa, but we always knew her as Clara."

Just then the woman in my head says, "See, I told you so, I told you they all knew me as Clara."

I don't know if you can imagine my shock. This was real! I had actually been speaking to a real person with a distinct personality, who happened to be in the spirit world. She had shown me that she was aware of events in her niece's life, and she even took advantage of the opportunity to say, "I told you so."

For me, this was another huge confirmation that the dead are still with us. This is one of the primary reasons why I encourage people to consciously develop their mediumship. When someone else is giving you a message you could always have some nagging question in the back of your mind about whether they were faking it in some way. But when you are the one talking directly to a person in spirit and giving a message to someone that you truly know nothing about, then you know it is real. In this case that I am describing, I had never met any of the people in the room. I certainly never knew that this woman had a great aunt named

Clara, so I knew I wasn't faking it.

This experience taught me something else as well: that spirit contact often feels just like you are just talking to yourself. Just like your normal internal dialogue. This got me wondering how many other times I had unknowingly spoken to people in the spirit world without realizing it. How many times when an idea or an answer to a question popped into my head was someone else feeding me the answer? Here all this time I just thought that I was brilliant, and it turns out that I'd probably been getting help all along.

Spontaneous mediumship

Almost everyone, at one time or another, has experienced what could be called "spontaneous mediumship." This is where you get a glimpse of something or someone, out of the corner of your eye - which then disappears when you look at it. It is when you hear a name called when no one is around, or get flashes of insight or sudden answers to questions. This is usually just a loved one from the other side trying to get your attention.

A surprising number of people have even experienced spontaneous physical mediumship in the form of odd rapping noises or the unexplained movement of inanimate objects. For someone who doesn't understand what is happening, these occurrences can be disturbing. Most people choose not to tell anyone about it out of fear of being considered odd, or even mentally ill (most people are very reluctant to admit that they have ever heard "voices").

But this is a natural skill that we all possess and which can be deliberately developed. In the rest of this book we will talk about how to consciously tap into this realm whenever you want to.

4

Clairvoyance

Psychic vs. medium

People sometimes confuse psychics and mediums. What is the difference? To put it simply, mediums talk to dead people to obtain the information that they give in a reading. Psychics read or sense the energy around a person or item to get their information. Generally all mediums are also psychic, while not all psychics are mediums.

So what is the difference between a psychic reading and a mediumistic reading? Well, if you want to make contact with a deceased loved one you would look for a mediumistic reading. Keep in mind that most of the information that the medium will give you will be based on what your loved one says to the medium. So if you are looking for advice about the stock market, for example, and you are talking to your deceased uncle Joe who knew nothing about the stock market, the advice you get is probably not going to be very good. He might mean well, but dying does not instantly make someone any smarter than they were in life. They often seem to have a longer or clearer view of issues than they did while alive, but they don't suddenly become authorities on everything. On the other hand, if your uncle was a great mechanic, he might have some very useful advice regarding the maintenance of your car.

Psychics, on the other hand, do not talk to dead people. Instead they sense the energy around a person. So if you want to know about your love life, the psychic can check to see if the energy around you feels positive or negative, and they can probably get a sense of what has happened to you lately in the romance department, and what is going to happen in the near future. They aren't, however, going to be able to get your deceased grandmother's opinion regarding your new boyfriend.

People usually go to psychics because they want to know what the future holds for them in the following five areas:

1) Money or job issues

2) Love issues (is the person I am dating the right one for me, when will I find the right partner, is my partner cheating on me, etc.)

3) Children issues (how many children am I going to have, is my teenager going to turn out alright)

4) Health issues (this is a tricky area because psychics are not allowed to diagnose or recommend treatment)

5) Honesty issues (is my business partner cheating me).

People usually go to mediums because they are grieving, they have unresolved issues with deceased loved ones, or they are looking for evidence that life goes on after death. However, as I pointed out, because mediums are also psychic, they will generally also be able to give you some advice about the five areas I mentioned in the previous paragraph.

The title and primary topic of this book is *"Help and Advice from the Other Side,"* so obviously most of what we are discussing in this book is mediumship.

Clear seeing

The term "clairvoyance" comes from the French word "clairvoyant" and means "clear seeing," or "clear sight," but it specifically refers to the ability to see objects, people or events that are not perceptible to the normal senses. This can include past, present, and future events. There are basically 2 types, or methods, of clairvoyance:

1) Direct clairvoyance is where you view events psychically without the use of any tools, just with your mind,

2) Clairvoyance with the help of tools.

Clairvoyance with the help of tools

Some people find it much easier, at least at first, to develop their psychic or mediumistic abilities with the help of tools. In Spiritualist churches you seldom see any public message work using tools (except for psychometry). Tools are seen as an unnecessary crutch. Most of what you see is mental mediumship. But for your own use I see no harm in using tools to help you develop.

1) Crystal or mirror gazing

One tool that is particularly easy to learn to use is the crystal ball or gazing mirror. Most people think of the image of an old gypsy fortune teller when they hear the term "crystal gazing." Crystal or mirror gazing, otherwise known as "scrying," is an excellent method for getting psychic impressions or having actual encounters with deceased loved ones.

Mirror gazing is one of my favorite techniques for getting messages for myself. It is the topic of my book *"Mirror Gazing: Predict the future, Look into the past, Unlock your creativity."* ISBN 978-1-926826-01-1. In this book I describe the uses of mirror gazing in much more detail, and give instructions on how to make your own black mirror gazing mirror out of an inexpensive picture frame.

The use of crystals, mirrors, or almost any object capable of presenting a reflective surface has been used all over the world throughout history as an aid to psychic vision. The mirror or the crystal effectively becomes the portal or doorway to other worlds. The tool acts merely to focus your attention. There is no particular virtue in any object used for this purpose. The "magic" is in you, not in the tool you use. However, the longer you use a particular gazing tool, the better it seems to work; so whatever tool you start off using will probably work even better over time.

Ideally, you should have your own mirror or crystal ball for your own use as this prevents cross contamination or the blending of vibratory influences from more than one person using the same tool. The tool should be put away between uses.

How to do it

You will need a quiet room where you can sit without being disturbed. Ideally it should be as free of distractions as possible. Basically, you set up the mirror, or crystal ball, or bowl of water, or whatever tool you want to use in front of you in a darkened room.

If you are using a crystal ball, you should surround the crystal with dark fabric to create a sensation of depth so that you are looking into the crystal, not through it. Any light source such as a candle should be beside or behind you, not reflecting into the surface of your scrying tool.

Scrying is generally a solitary activity, but if you do have another person in the room with you, they need to stay silent and remain seated at a distance.

If you have some meditation music that you find relaxing, you can put it on to help get you in the mood. You can open with a prayer if you like, then relax in your chair and gaze calmly at the reflective surface. Don't strain your eyes, and don't try to avoid blinking your eyes. Just sit and watch the reflective surface with relaxed expectation. Don't try to will something to happen: simply wait and see.

Scrying is basically a form of self-induced hypnosis. You are putting yourself into a light trance state. We all go in and out of light trance states several times a day. We are all capable of doing it. The darkened room and lack of visual sensory input create what is known as the "Ganzfeld effect" or "prisoner's cinema" which is where the mind begins to compensate for the lack of visual stimulation by creating something.

What will you see?

What usually happens is that after a time you will begin to see a cloudy, milky mist appear. Simply acknowledge in your mind that you have seen it and wait to see what else happens. Usually, the cloud formation becomes denser and then it begins to clear and other images begin to appear.

A variety of things can take place on the blank surface of the scrying tool. The images you see will either be symbolic, or actual scenes or persons. You might see still pictures, like looking through a photo album, or moving pictures, like watching a movie on a television. The moving images might appear to come out of the tool and take place with you in the room, or if you are really lucky you might find yourself effectively being sucked into the tool and participating in the action inside it.

Scrying can be a very effective tool for actually being able to visit with deceased loved ones or historical figures.

How long should you sit?

You can sit as long as you are comfortable and relaxed. Once you start noticing your butt, the session is pretty well over. Generally sessions last somewhere between 15 minutes and one hour. Once you have had enough you will simply come out of your self-induced trance state and the session will be over.

2) Tea leaf reading

This is another technique that anyone can learn. It is the topic of my book *"Messages in Your Tea Cup: Learn to read tea leaves."* ISBN 978-0-9783939-6-0.

Basically you relax by drinking a cup of tea made using loose tea, and when you finish drinking the liquid you gaze into the tealeaves that are left in your cup. Our minds are always trying to make sense of, or see patterns out of, random shapes, so you will soon begin to see images appearing in the bottom of the cup. Don't analyze it too carefully; just blurt out the first thing you see. In tea leaf reading, the images will always be symbolic. See the image, and then ask yourself what that image symbolizes to you. For example, if you see a bell, is it a church bell, which might symbolize marriage? Or is it a school bell which could symbolize childhood or that you will be going back to school?

In tea leaf reading you are not directly speaking to a deceased loved one, but if it is your intent, and if they are willing, they can put the ideas for what you are seeing directly into your mind in this way.

3) Psychometry

This is where you "read," or sense, the energy of an object. In psychometry you are using a physical object to provide a connecting link to a person, place, or time. People often attempt to use psychometry to locate missing persons. This is sometimes referred to as getting the "psychic scent" from the item. Similar to the way search and rescue dogs can follow a person's trail by sniffing a piece of clothing, a psychic can get "the psychic scent" of an event from the energy around an item. But psychometry can also be a tool for mediums. In the first chapter of this book, I described how a medium used psychometry to make contact with my father and grandmother.

But psychometry is not only used to make contact with people; it can also be used to look at historical events that took place around the item. The physical object carries along with it, in its inner substance or nature, the vibrations of its past environment. The clairvoyant is then able to follow the psychic "scent" until they establish a connection with the distant object, person, or scene associated with the physical object.

William Walker Atkinson, in his book *"Mediumship,"* described how he brought a tiny fragment of stone, not larger than a pin's head, from Stonehenge, and put it into an envelope and handed it to a psychometrist who had no idea what it was. Upon touching the envelope she was able to describe Stonehenge and the desolate country surrounding it, and then went on to describe scenes from its early history. This convinced him that, in spite of the tiny size of the fragment, the piece of stone had within it the "memory" of everything that had taken place there.

Although I've never tried it for this purpose, apparently psychometry can be used effectively to prospect for gold, other minerals, or oil. A psychometrist can follow up the psychic "scent" of a piece of stone and "examine" underground conditions at the place where the stone was taken from, and describe the conditions lying underground.

Letters, clothes, hair, coins, ornaments, or jewels - in fact, almost any article which has belonged to or has been worn by its possessor for any length of time can be used to get impressions. Some people find that they have more success with certain kinds of objects than with others.

Because old furniture, old pictures, and old jewelry often carry with them the memories of past people, places, and events associated with the item, wandering through antique stores can be an interesting way to practice. The only problem with practicing in an antique store is that you probably won't be able to confirm whether your impressions are correct.

William Walker Atkinson in his book *"Mediumship"* described an interesting example of using a letter to perform psychometry:

> *"One of the most interesting experiments I ever witnessed in Psychometry was that in which a letter that had been forwarded from place to place, until it had gone completely around the globe, was psychometrized by a young Hindu maid. Although ignorant of the outside world of foreign lands, the young woman was able to picture the people and scenery of every part of the globe in which the letter had traveled. Her report was really an interesting 'travelogue' of a trip around the world, given in tabloid form."*

How to do it

Psychometry is simple to describe, but not so simple to do. For most people it requires a lot of practice.

You clear your mind of all your personal thoughts, touch the item (if it is small enough, some people like to hold the item up to their forehead), and wait to see if you get an impression of something or someone. If the conditions are right, you will begin to have flashes of scenes associated with the history of the object in question. Once you get and acknowledge your first impression, subsequent, more in-depth, impressions will come to you. At first these impressions may be somewhat disconnected and confused, but before long the mental picture will become clearer. Most people keep their eyes closed when practicing psychometry in order to allow their inner senses to function without distraction from the outer senses.

"Confused" impressions

Sometimes when an item has been handled by a lot of people, or has passed from one owner to another throughout its history, you can get a blending of vibratory influences. In cases like this, the psychometrist is unable to sense each distinct influence causing a "confused" reading. For best results, try to avoid having too many people handling a particular item prior to a psychometry session.

Direct clairvoyance

Direct clairvoyance (clear seeing) is where you attempt to make a mental connection with persons in spirit without the use of a tool. Generally, when we talk about mediumship, we are talking about direct clairvoyance. This is where you attempt to raise your psychic vibrations so as to become "in tune" with the higher vibrations of those who have crossed over to the spirit world; actually, it is more like the two of you meet in the middle. It is not usually possible for people to cross over back and forth; you just meet in something of a middle ground. The only exception to this is in the case of Shaman who claim to be able to move back and forth between worlds.

Other forms of direct clairvoyance include remote viewing (which is a psychic skill rather than a mediumistic skill) and inspired writing (which involves spirit contact and is therefore mediumistic).

Remote viewing

Being able to perform remote viewing is like having an "x-ray sense." It enables the psychic to see through a brick wall or any other physical obstacle. The distance from the objects, persons, scenes, or events being perceived is irrelevant. It is just as easy to see clairvoyantly over the space of a thousand miles, as over a few hundred feet - the principle involved is exactly the same.

Sometimes the view of a distant scene obtained in this way is similar to that seen through a telescope. Human figures can appear very small, like watching something on a distant stage. However, in spite of their diminutive size they are as clear as though they were close by. Sometimes it is possible to hear what is said as well as to see what is done. Other times it feels as though the observer is physically present at the location, everything is life-sized, and you can even feel, hear, and smell the surroundings. However, even though it might feel that you are physically present you have not actually left your physical body at all.

Inspired writing

In inspired writing, a spirit impresses the message upon the mind of the medium, and the medium writes out the message. Music and poetry are often created this way. The medium is aware of what he is about to write. The medium retains control of his writing muscles, and the spirit merely places the thought into the mind of the medium. The writing style is usually a blending of that of the spirit's style and the medium's style, and the personality of the medium subtly influences the message. This is different from automatic writing (which is covered in the chapter on physical mediumship) where the spirit takes over control of the medium's writing muscles and the medium is unaware of what is being written. In automatic writing the personality of the medium plays no part whatsoever.

Meditation for mediumship development

Going into a trance is not necessary for mediumship. What most mediums are actually doing could better be thought of as deep concentration. They are shutting out the sounds, sights, and thoughts of the outside world around them and concentrating their full attention upon the clairvoyant work inside them. This could perhaps be considered a semi-trance state.

What you need to do is learn how to focus your consciousness to a single point, to become "one pointed," as the Hindu teachers call it. We do this all the time naturally. We easily concentrate our full attention when we are watching an interesting movie or reading an enthralling book. In these cases our attention is completely occupied with the interesting thing before us, so that we have almost completely shut out the outer world of sound, sight, and thought, but we are, nevertheless, perfectly wide awake and conscious.

Anyone who is serious about developing mediumship would be wise to take up the practice of daily meditation. Most people, when they think of meditation, think of Buddhist monks or Hindu holy men, sitting quietly in uncomfortable positions for long periods of time, but that is very difficult for most people and fortunately is not the only way to meditate.

Learning to gain control of your thoughts is very difficult for most people in our society. Meditation is not so much about emptying your mind of all thoughts; that is almost impossible. It could more accurately be described as being totally focused on what you are doing at the moment. Most of the time, we are living in the past and in the future, and not in the present. We usually miss so much of what we are experiencing right now.

As we saw earlier in this book, the mind is a very powerful tool that most people have not learned to master. The goal is to always be aware of exactly what we are thinking about so that we can use our mind effectively, and turn it on, focus it, or hold it still at will. The easiest way of doing this is to make an effort to be consciously aware of what you are thinking about. It is not necessary to be seated quietly to do this. We should be doing this throughout the day no matter where we are or what we are doing.

If you are playing with your child, be totally focused on playing with your child; don't be thinking about what you are going to make for dinner. If you are writing a letter, think of nothing but the letter until it is finished. If you are reading a book, keep your mind on the book; don't let it wander off. Be present in the moment.

This is the most important thing that you can do because when you have trained your mind to stay focused on what you are doing at the moment, when you want to focus on speaking to people in spirit you will not find your mind wandering off in other directions.

Training the mind

It has often been said that the mind is like a spoiled two-year-old when his mother is on the phone, constantly wanting attention. The minute you sit down to meditate, a million other thoughts jump into your attention. Suddenly you find yourself thinking about what to make for dinner, an incident that took place in the third grade, or you get a sudden urge to get up and pay the phone bill. If you do manage to calm your mind for a moment then your body gets involved, and suddenly you develop an irritating itch, your butt goes numb, or you find yourself yawning.

As any mother of a two-year-old soon discovers, it is futile to attempt to force matters. Distraction is the answer. These following exercises are the equivalent of giving a child a cookie or a coloring book and crayons.

Monkey mind

In Buddhism the tendency of our mind to jump around frantically from one thought to another is sometimes referred to as "monkey mind." You control monkey mind by giving your conscious mind something to focus on.

Exercises that you can do to control your mind

It is not absolutely necessary to do any of these exercises in order to develop mediumship, but if you want to improve your visualization skills or simply learn how to relax, you can do these exercises at random times throughout the day when you have a few free minutes. They are particularly effective in increasing your ability to stay focused on one particular thought and thereby controlling monkey mind. If you just have fun and don't struggle with these exercises you will find them very relaxing. Regardless of how badly you think you are doing at first, as time goes on you will be amazed at your progress.

Simple objects

This is a very easy exercise that you can do anytime that you have a minute or two when you can close your eyes. There are no other props or tools required for this one.

Simply sit down, relax, and look at some object near you. It doesn't matter what the object is. For example, right now as I sit here at my computer desk there are numerous items that I can choose from: a pen, the desk lamp, my water bottle, the phone. What you choose doesn't matter. Just get it firmly in your mind and then close your eyes. With your eyes closed "visualize" the object. If you find that you can't "see" it, just open your eyes and take another look at it.

Once you can do that easily you can progress to altering the appearance of the object. Make it bigger or smaller. Distort it and then bring it back to its original shape. Change the color. Just play with it.

Morphing shapes

This exercise is a progression from the simple objects exercise. In this case you do not have an item in front of you to look at; it exists only in your mind. It is a bit like a screen saver I used to have on my computer.

Simply close your eyes, relax, and "see" a square. Make the square large and then smaller, distort it, turn it into a diamond shape then back into a square. Make it three-dimensional by turning it into a cube. Stretch it out and turn it into a rectangle.

Experiment with colors, make it red, orange, yellow, green, blue, purple. Make each side a different color, and then blur the colors into each other. Spin the shape around slowly, then faster, and then slow it down again.

Soften the edges, morph the shape into a circle, then make it three dimensional and turn it into a ball, make the ball spin, then bounce, color it in solid colors, then into patterns.

Experiment with different shapes, morph one into the next, first a square, then a triangle, then add sides, first 5 sides, then 6 sides, then 7 sides, then 8. Smooth the 8 sides into a circle, and then turn it into an oval, and back into a square. See how smooth and seamless the transitions can become.

This is a great game to play when you are at the dentist, or during other minor medical procedures. When you are able to focus completely on the morphing shapes you will be amazed to find that you don't notice any discomfort.

Rose bud

Once you become adept at visualizing simple objects and morphing shapes you can try this rose bud exercise. This is the first exercise that involves the sense of smell and touch.

Close your eyes and imagine a tightly closed rose bud. "See" the stem, the thorns, and the leaves. "See" the color of the petals, notice how the green of the stem is lighter in some places and darker in others, blending to almost yellow at the point of the thorns.

Watch as the rose bud begins to slowly loosen, then each petal begins to open up. Notice the way the color of the petals seems darker toward the center, and lighter toward the tips.

When the rose is fully open, smell the beautiful fragrance, and feel the velvety softness of the petals against your cheek.

Experiment with opening up the rose bud then closing it back up again a few times, then open the rose up fully and watch it begin to droop, watch the petals turn darker and the edges curl, and then one by one they fall off, leaving just the rose hip in the center.

If you get really good at this, you can try reversing the process. Re-create the rose, starting with just the rose hip and watch the petals go back into place, watch the curled edges straighten out, see the color come back. Then watch the petals as they tighten back into a rose bud.

Morphing numbers

This one is similar to the morphing shapes exercise. If you are an analytical type person who likes to measure your progress you will like this one. For this exercise you will need a minute timer, a piece of paper and a pen or pencil.

Set the timer for either 1 or 2 minutes. It is amazing how long 2 minutes can seem when you first begin.

Close your eyes and "see" the number 1. Write it out in your mind as though you were writing it on a piece of paper, then watch it morph into a three dimensional shape. Then do the same thing with the number 2, then 3, and on and on.

Every time that you get distracted and fail to keep the number clearly in your mind, you have to start again at number one. When the timer goes off, write down the number you got to. As time goes on you can increase the timer to 5 minutes, then 10 minutes.

Your progress in this will seem sporadic. Some days you will do better than others. Don't stress yourself over your apparent lack of progress. Over time you will improve.

If you don't have a minute timer, a variation on this exercise is to record the time when you begin and then keep going until you reach a particular number, perhaps 30 to begin with. Same as previously, every time you get distracted and lose the number you start again from 1. When you finally reach your goal number, open your eyes and record the time. Gradually you will find that you can reach your goal number faster and faster.

If, at first, you find that variation too difficult, you can simply record the time that you start and then go as far as you can before you get distracted. Then simply open your eyes and record the time and the number that you reached.

I like the challenge aspect of this number exercise, but if you find yourself getting stressed about wanting to "succeed" and feel bad about your apparent lack of progress, then forget it and use the other exercises instead!

Walking or exercise as meditation

Simply going out for a long walk can be a form of meditation. I also find that bicycling or paddling a canoe over long distances can be meditative. The rhythm and repetition helps to quiet your mind, and enables you to quiet your inner dialogue.

Everyone meditates to some degree whether we realize it or not. Even sitting in front of the television set is a form of meditation. Unfortunately, in this case you are putting yourself into a relaxed meditative state and filling your mind with whatever is on television. I think it is far better to control what you allow into your mind.

"There are no miracles.
Everything that happens is the result of law --
eternal, immutable, ever active."

Madame Blavatsky

5

Psychic Readings

The primary focus of this book is mediumship, which is the ability to connect with individuals who have crossed over - in other words, people who have died. However, it is also possible to get a lot of information by "reading" the energy around living people. This is what people refer to when they talk about "psychic" readings.

Some people think that you need to obtain access to the Universal Consciousness or Divine Mind to get a vision of past or future events, but this is not necessarily so. In psychic readings we are reading the residual energy of the person, place, or event. For example, if you have a little electric heater in a room, but then move it to another room, the heat remains in the first room until it gradually dissipates. Likewise, when a person wearing cologne leaves a room, the odor still lingers. The wake of a ship is often visible for hours after the ship has passed from sight. In other words, the cause may be gone, but the effect remains. Similarly, human beings have energy fields surrounding them, and leave residual energy when they leave exit a room.

Human energy fields

There are energies constantly surrounding us which are invisible to normal sight but which can be "read" by people who have developed the ability. These energies can tell us a lot about a person.

Have you ever met someone and instantly felt that you liked or disliked them? Without realizing it, you might instinctively be picking up information from their aura.

The human aura

The human aura is the psychic atmosphere that surrounds the human body. We all have an aura. It is an egg-shaped, hazy looking substance, which surrounds the person for two or three feet around the body. It is most dense near the body, and gradually becomes less dense the farther it extends away from the body.

The aura is composed of all the colors of the spectrum, the combination shifting with the person's changing mental and emotional state. Everyone has their own distinctive auric colors, depending upon their character or personality. Each mental or emotional state is reflected by its own particular shade or combination of shades of colors. As a result, a person's character can be evaluated by studying their aura.

You can feel or sense a person's aura even if you can't consciously see it; so don't feel that because you don't see the colors, you can't do psychic readings. Most people "feel" the colors or the shape of the aura without ever seeing them.

The human aura is not a stationary bubble, it is continually moving and shifting and changing colors, sometimes shooting out toward the objects the person is attracted to. Other times the aura seems to pull in and condense. During periods of emotional upheaval, the aura appears to swirl around, shooting out and pulling back, throwing forth tiny sparks of psychic vibrations that can travel great distances.

The colors of the aura

The colors of a person's aura are constantly changing as the person's thoughts and feelings change, so it is impossible for a person to completely conceal the real state of their feelings on any subject.

Generally, bright colors indicate good energy and good health, while dark, muddy colors indicate problems, either emotional (for example fear or resentment) or physical (health problems).

What the different colors of the aura represent depends on the perception of the viewer. The following are some general guidelines when interpreting the meanings of colors, but don't bother trying to memorize these meanings because when you see or feel a color you will also sense the meaning of the color as well.

Aura color interpretations

Red

The color red either attracts or repels. When clear and bright, it represents power, energy, competition, sex, and passion. Lots of bright red in the aura indicates that the person is strong willed and active. When dark and muddy, it can represent anger, anxiety, money worries, or obsessions. Being the color of blood, it can refer to the physical body, such as the heart or the circulatory system.

Pink

Bright, light pink indicates a person who is loving, tender, sensitive, sensual, artistic, affectionate, and compassionate. It can also indicate that the person is involved in a new romantic relationship. It can also indicate clairaudience. A muddy pink indicates problems involving love.

Orange

Orange is the color of vitality, good health and excitement. Lots of orange in an aura means that the person is energetic and has plenty of stamina; they are courageous adventurous, and outgoing. A muddy orange color indicates a feeling of frustration and a sense of being held back.

Yellow

Yellow is the color of intelligence, inspiration, creativity, playfulness, and optimism. It indicates emerging psychic and spiritual awareness, optimism and hopefulness, and new ideas. A dark muddy yellow often indicates someone who is straining at studying and is feeling fatigued or stressed; someone who is trying to do everything at once.

Green

Green is the healthy color of nature. When seen in the aura, this usually represents growth, balance, and change. The person is a healer and has a love of people, animals, and nature. A dark muddy green can represent jealousy, resentment, feeling like a victim, blaming others, insecurity and low self-esteem, lack of personal responsibility, and sensitivity to perceived criticism.

Blue

The color blue often relates to the throat, either physically, as in a physical issue with the throat, or symbolically, as in speaking your mind. Emotionally, the color blue is calm, cool and collected. It represents caring, loving, helping others, intuition, and clarity in communication. A lot of bright blue in the aura indicates a person who is truthful, intuitive, generous, and highly spiritual. A muddy blue represents a fear of facing or speaking the truth, or fear of the future.

Violet/Purple/Lavender

Violet or purple are the intuitive colors in the aura, revealing psychic power and attunement. The most sensitive and wisest of colors, it can indicate a visionary, idealistic, artistic, imaginative person with a tendency to daydream.

Silver

Silver is the color of abundance, both spiritual and physical. Lots of bright silver in the aura can represent plenty of money, or the awakening of the spiritual nature. A dark muddy gray represents fear and potential financial problems.

Gold

Gold is the color of enlightenment and divine protection. Its presence in the aura indicates divine guidance, protection, wisdom, and inner knowledge.

Black

The color black in an aura usually indicates a long-term inability to forgive others, or past painful situations which have not been released. It can also indicate depression, anger and feelings of revenge.

White

White in the aura represents purity and truth, or new spiritual energy. White sparkles or flashes of white light mean that angels are nearby. It can sometimes indicate that the person is pregnant or will be expecting shortly.

Rainbows

Rainbows shooting out from the hands, head or body indicates someone who is a healer.

Pastel colors

Pastel colors rather than deep, intense colors indicate that the person is very sensitive and needs plenty of quiet time and serenity.

Exercise to develop your ability to "feel" colors

One of the best ways to learn how to feel the essence of a color is to practice touching colors and seeing how they make you feel.

Take small pieces of solid colored fabric or construction paper. Pick up each colored piece separately, look at it, and then close your eyes and sense it. Then put all of the colored pieces into a bag, and with your eyes closed pull one out at a time and sense the color. With practice you will be able to tell what color it is just by feel.

This is an excellent exercise to do with a partner.

The prana aura

The prana aura is sometimes called the health aura. For many people the prana aura is an easier version of the aura to see initially. It is colorless, but still apparent, sort of like looking through clear glass or water. It is like seeing vibrating heated air arising from a hot stove, or from hot pavement in summertime. To see it, simply close your eyes partially, and peer through your narrowed eyelids. You will be able to see this prana aura surrounding the body of a person, especially if the person is standing in a dim light against a solid, dark background. The prana aura contains very tiny, bristle-like lines. If the individual is in good health these fine lines are stiff like toothbrush bristles; while in the case of poor health these lines droop, curl, and appear wilted. It is sometimes filled with tiny sparkling particles, which vibrate and move about.

The easiest way to train yourself to see the prana aura is to hold up your hand against a dark background, in a dim light. Then gaze at your fingers through narrowed eyelids. After a little practice, you will begin to see a fine thin line, or a haze, surrounding your fingers on all sides, similar to the radiance surrounding a candle flame. In most cases this border of aura is colorless. The stronger the energy surrounding a person, the stronger and brighter will this border of prana aura appear.

Thought forms

Every thought or emotion has its own rate of vibration, and this vibration creates a vibratory "form" that can be seen or felt. These thought-forms vary according to the type of thought that created it. Some appear like a faint wave similar to the tiny waves caused by dropping a pebble in a pool of water. Others are more like a whirlpool, rotating and whirling in space. Others appear more like exploding bombs. Others branch out arms like an octopus wriggling in all directions, trying to attach themselves to some other person or object.

Reading past or future energy

In addition to reading the energy around a person in the present, it is possible to perceive the energy of objects, persons, scenes, and events from the past or future time. In other words, it is possible to read the energy of things which existed in the physical world in times past, which have long since vanished from physical existence; or the energy belonging to future events.

It is just as easy for a clairvoyant to see things and events occurring five thousand years ago as it is to see things occurring one week ago. The principle involved is the same.

Thousand-year-old light

Light travels at the rate of 186,000 miles per second. A "light-year," refers to the distance traveled by a light wave during the period of one of our earth years. Some distant stars are estimated to be more than one thousand light-years away from us. The light we now perceive as coming from them is actually the light that left them more than one thousand years ago. So, if one of these stars was destroyed today, we would not become aware of it for a thousand years. In fact, the star whose light we see now may actually no longer exist, because it may have been destroyed years ago. Other stars are closer to us, but the principle is the same. We see the stars not as they are at the present moment, but as they were when the light left them, perhaps many years ago. Thus, we are actually perceiving the events long after they happened. The record of these past events are present in these light waves. Every event that has ever taken place is recorded in light waves.

The Akashic records

However, viewing events in the past is not always dependent upon seeing the light-waves as they pass by. The "Astral Plane," or the "Akashic Plane", contains traces and impressions of all the happenings of the past on the earth. These Akashic records have sometimes been referred to as "the memory of the earth." Sometimes clairvoyants are able to access these Akashic records and thereby view past events. Many psychics are unaware of the existence of the Akashic records, even though they regularly view them. They simply know that they are able to "see" these past happenings without having the faintest idea of how they are able to see them.

One thing to keep in mind is that you are not seeing the actual event; rather, you are seeing a reflection of the event, similar to viewing a scene reflected into the troubled waters of a lake. Sometimes the water is calm and you can see more clearly than other times, but there is almost always some element of error or distorted reflection.

Keep in mind that every vision is not necessarily a picture from the Akashic records, nor every experience a revelation from on high. It is far better to err on the side of healthy skepticism than that of over-credulity; and never hunt for a mysterious occult explanation of anything when a plain and obvious physical one is available.

Doing psychic readings through psychometry

Psychometry involves touching an item and reading its energy to get information about past events. While it is possible, as I mentioned in chapter 1, to use psychometry to connect with the spirit world, it can be used very effectively to read past events psychically. Since the residual energy of previous people or events often still lingers on the item, it is just a matter of clearing your mind and allowing yourself to sense the residue attached to the item. We all have this ability, but most of the time we shut it down to prevent being bombarded with too much information. One way to develop this skill is to spend time in antique or second hand stores touching the items and being consciously aware of the impressions that you get.

The mystery of time - the eternal now

We can easily grasp the idea that it is possible to see events in the past through their lingering traces, but how do we explain the ability to see events that have not yet taken place, events in the future? Quantum physics suggests that time is just a relative mode of regarding things. We experience our lives at a certain definite pace, and we interpret this as if the events were moving in this order and at this precise rate. But that may be only one way of looking at things. Quantum theory suggests that events may be in some sort of existence always, both past and future, and it may be we who are arriving at them, not they that are happening in sequence. Consider the analogy of a train traveler. If the traveler could never leave the train (in other words, never had the experience of getting off the train and remaining stationary), and could not alter the train's direction or pace, the traveler might think of the landscapes that the train passes through as successive, and be unable to conceive that all of the landscapes are actually coexisting all at the same time.

Hindu philosophy has an explanation of time that is based upon the idea that everything, past, present, and future, was created by a Supreme Being in a single moment of time. In other words, that to the Supreme Being, all the past, all the present, all the future of the universe, are but a single thought in a single moment of time - an instantaneous act of consciousness. Looked at this way, there is a possible fourth dimensional aspect about time, the eternal now, a single unit of conscious experience - an infinitesimal point of time in eternity.

This is all just speculation for us as human beings, kind of like ants on a golf course speculating about how space travel works. We can come up with possible explanations but we probably don't have the perspective to really be able to understand it. How or why it is possible to predict future events is unknown, but it does work, even if it doesn't work perfectly every time.

Why doesn't it work every time?

I suspect that there are some things that we just are not meant to know in advance. I think that our lives are meant to be adventures, or mystery novels, and to get all the information in advance would spoil the surprise. Besides, I am of the opinion that if I can't do anything to prevent something bad from happening, then I don't want to know about it in advance, but if there is something bad that can be prevented, then I want to know how.

Cause and effect

Finally, keep in mind that sometimes a prophecy of coming events is not true clairvoyance at all, but simply the subconscious workings of the mind. The amazing supercomputer that is our mind can take a strong existing cause, and can reason out the probable effect (the almost certain effect, in fact) of that cause, even though that effect lies far in the future. The subconscious mind works upon the principle that "coming events cast their shadows before." But this is not true clairvoyance - it is merely the statement of "probable" results, and effects of existing causes. But a thousand-and-one unforeseen things may arise to completely upset the prediction, for it is never actually true until it occurs.

*"Death is no more than
passing from one room into another. But
there's a difference for me, you know. Because
in that other room I shall be able to see."*

Helen Keller

6

Mediumship

What is mediumship?

The word "medium" means something that lies in the middle, or between other things, a conduit through which something is conveyed from one place to another. So in Spiritualism, a "medium" is someone who acts as a channel of communication between discarnate (spirit) entities and human beings that are still in the flesh.

The term "discarnate" means away from the physical body, or out of the flesh. In other words "discarnate" beings are spirits, or people who have died, or perhaps have never even lived as humans in the flesh. Communication with discarnate entities has been known and practiced from the earliest days of recorded history. The Hebrew Scriptures contain many instances of such communication, showing that contact with the spirit world was an accepted fact of life at the time and in the places where the Bible was written.

Keep in mind that although these spirit beings do not have a physical body like we do, they seem to occupy a body composed of some sort of ethereal substance. This ethereal body is sometimes called the "astral body," or the "spiritual body." This is how, under certain circumstances, we are able to see them and how, as in the example that I mentioned at the beginning of this book where my father showed his legs to the medium, the medium was able to see the legs that my father was showing him.

Mediumship does not depend upon any particular form of religious belief, or teaching, and does not require the acceptance of any one particular religious belief. In other words, you don't have to believe in Spiritualism to make a connection with those in spirit. All that is required is that you be willing to entertain the idea that the human soul persists after the death of the body. My reason for saying that you have to be "willing to entertain the idea" is that if you refuse to even consider the idea that the dead live on, you will never make contact. You have to at least believe it is possible, even if you are not initially totally convinced.

We are immortal

As we will see throughout the rest of this book, there are many forms of spirit manifestation, and we can certainly take advantage of spirit assistance to enhance our lives on earth, but the primary purpose of all forms of mediumship is to bring positive proof of the continuation of life after death. In other words, what mediumship does is prove to us that we are immortal. We all will eventually discard our physical bodies, but we will continue to exist, and continue to have our own unique personality.

Mediums, acting as intermediaries, enable those in spirit to comfort the grieving, and give advice to those in need. Our present day experiences of spirit manifestation prove, or explain, many things that are recorded in ancient records. Spiritualism explains many of the supposedly "supernatural" events of the Bible. It also explains the ability, claimed by the ancient prophets, to see angels and hear voices. We now know that it is a natural ability which happens spontaneously for some people, while for the rest of us it requires practice.

Once you become convinced of the truth of the personal

survival of your loved ones, you realize that there is nothing to fear in death, and you then understand that the heaven and hell of orthodox Christianity are concepts that were misinterpreted and used to control the masses of the public. Once you have experienced for yourself that communication between the two worlds is real, all religious condemnation of the practice, or charges of fraud against mediums, becomes irrelevant.

Who can become a medium?

Anyone can develop the ability to connect with those in spirit. It is a natural ability that we all possess. It doesn't matter if you are male or female, young or old.

Some people claim that you have to become something of an aesthetic, eating health food, practicing yoga, and meditating for hours on end to become truly adept at mediumship, and I know some great mediums that are like this. But some of the greatest mediums in history have been very much the opposite. Substance abuse has run rampant throughout the recorded history of mediumship. So this is promising for those of us who fall somewhere in between the two extremes.

One thing that I have been dismayed to discover is that you don't necessarily have to be a kind, loving, spiritually minded person to become a medium. I have run across a few very unkind, unethical people who are able to function as very competent mediums. This baffled me at first, but I have come to the conclusion that when I meet someone who falls into this category (and I really haven't run across very many of them), that there is just something about their life or their spiritual development that I just don't understand, and that is none of my concern.

What matters to me is that I personally endeavor to behave in an honest, ethical manner and represent mediumship and Spiritualism to the best of my ability.

Higher vibrations

So, if spirit communication is normal and natural, why isn't it easier to do? Why does there seem to be a curtain or veil between us? I am not absolutely certain, but it seems to have something to do with the fact that those in the spirit world are not constrained by physical bodies like we are, and it is believed that their world vibrates at a much higher rate than our own earth-plane. As a result their communication is at a higher frequency or rate than ours and we do not ordinarily register and interpret these higher vibrations of communication. Therefore, for us to recognize their higher frequency we have to raise our own vibrations to "catch" these higher vibrations.

Psychic attunement

While we on the earth plane (those of us who are living) have to learn how to fine tune our ability to connect, those in spirit who want to communicate with the living also have some adjusting and learning to do. I am convinced that some spirits are just better at it than others, and some probably just don't bother to learn. I can't prove it, but I think that this is why it is easier to get a clearer connection from some spirits than from others.

Also, some people just seem to click. You know how it is when you meet someone new on the earth plane, sometimes you just connect with new people right away, you understand each other; the two of you really communicate, while with other people you just don't. The same is true with people who have crossed over, some spirit people you connect with well, while with others you just don't seem to click.

Spirit guides

So what seems to happen when you develop mediumship is that you connect with one or two particular people on the spirit side who act as your intermediaries. These are people in spirit that you connect well with, and they help assist the others in spirit in getting their messages through to you. It usually takes some practice, some trial and error, between you and your spirit guides to learn what works best for the two of you.

But sometimes, no matter how hard you both try, you just don't work well together and you need to change guides. This is frustrating for you, and probably equally frustrating for the spirit guide, so if it just isn't working simply ask them to find you someone else that you can connect with more easily. It's not like you are "firing" them, they don't seem to take it personally, and I suspect that the guides that you "fire" still hang around to help the new guides make the connection with you.

Crowd control

There are so many people on the other side who would dearly love to make contact with their living loved ones that sometimes, when you first attempt to make contact, it feels like there are crowds of people trying to talk to you at once. The messages get all jumbled, you get part of a message from one person combined with bits and pieces from other people, and nothing seems to make sense to the person you are giving the message to. So part of your spirit guide's job is crowd control. Basically they are responsible for making the people in spirit line up and wait their turn.

When you first begin doing public message work, this jumbling of messages sometimes takes place. You might be giving a message to one particular person in the audience and spirit people and information for a person sitting next to them keeps popping in. Keeping them separate does get easier with practice, but regardless of how much experience you have, every medium experiences it on occasion.

Your guides are also responsible for finding the spirit people that you are trying to contact. Some people call these spirits who run around getting the spirits lined up for their turn "runner guides." I don't usually use that expression, but if you hear a medium referring to their "runner guides," you will know what they are talking about.

Also, as I mentioned earlier, your guides are responsible for facilitating communication. In other words, they relay messages from spirit people who don't seem to be very good communicators.

Mental mediumship vs. physical mediumship

Most mediumship performed today is what is referred to as "mental" mediumship. Physical mediumship was big in the 1800's, in the early days of Spiritualism.

Earlier in this chapter, I mentioned that anyone can become a medium, but where physical mediumship is concerned, one particular body type seems to have an advantage. Most of the old time physical mediums tended to be heavy individuals, with a large amount of abdominal fat. In other words, this is about the only time that I can think of where being fat seems to be an advantage.

Why is this the case? I am not exactly sure, although some people claim that it has to do with the body's ability to generate ectoplasm. But I will explain all about ectoplasm when I go into more detail about physical mediumship in chapter 10.

Is it necessary to go into a trance?

Some people are under the impression that it is necessary to go into a trance state in order to perform mental mediumship, but in spite of what we see in movies and television, this is not the case. While it is true that some mediums do lapse into a sort of light trance (I would describe it more as a "distracted" state where they are paying more attention to the spirit world than to the world around them), most appear to be in a perfectly normal, waking condition.

Many of the best mediums in the world have never been entranced in the sense of being in an unconscious sleep. The Fox sisters, and most of the other original rapping mediums, were never in a deep sleep trance. True, there have been some famous trance mediums such as Edgar Cayce, Nettie Colburn, and Euspasia Paladino who did their work when in a trance. In their cases, it seems that the more complete the trance, the more striking the results produced, but generally it is not necessary.

Unconscious mediumship

Spirit influence is not limited to those who are consciously attempting to be mediums. All of us are in contact with those in the spirit world all of the time, it is just that most of the time we are not consciously aware of it. We think the ideas that pop into our heads are our own, spontaneous impulses, which we act upon and reap the benefits. But I am convinced that if we get an idea that we can neither explain, nor trace its source, then someone on the spirit side probably put it there to help us.

We can take advantage of their willingness to help if, instead of being frightened by the idea of mental contact with spirit, we accept that such assistance from the other side is perfectly natural and can be very helpful. Turning this sort of unconscious mediumship into something that we consciously use for our benefit is discussed later in the chapter on spirit mentors.

Mediumship is not dangerous

From my own experiences, and those of the many mediums that I know well, I can say with absolute conviction that there is nothing dangerous in mental mediumship. So there is no need to perform special "protection" rituals. Yes, it is true that you are opening yourself up to connection with the spirit world, but all of us are in regular contact with that world whether we realize it or not. Also, it is important to remember that we are in control of the situation. Those in spirit do not control us, so there is no danger of getting "possessed." So, in spite of scenes that horror stories like "The Exorcist" portray, you will not lose your individuality or your self-control.

Even though it is not dangerous, dabbling in mediumship, for excitement, or to gratify your ego, is not a great idea. I'm sure you have heard the expression, "like attracts like," which simply means that you attract to yourself the people and events that are harmonious with you. So if you are just "fooling around," you will attract to yourself those on the spirit side who are also just "fooling around" and the results will probably not be what you are hoping for.

Generally, when we are endeavoring to connect with those on the other side, we are attempting to connect with our departed loved ones, or someone who has some particular expertise whose advice we want. In these cases, the results are almost invariably beneficial.

Domineering or "trickster" spirits

Spirits do not expect you to surrender your skepticism, or your ability to reason. On the contrary, they expect you to test to make sure that they are who they say they are. They will not be insulted. Every new idea that they give you should be evaluated, and rejected if it does not make sense to you.

However, just as there are domineering, opinionated people on the earth plane, there are also such people on the spirit side. Their personality does not suddenly become reasonable and helpful just because they have left their physical bodies. If you do run across such a domineering spirit, someone who demands unquestioning compliance with their commands, simply say a polite "no thanks" and effectively hang up the phone and don't call them again. Ask for someone else next time, someone that you can work with.

Occasionally you will run across a "trickster" spirit, someone who is just playing around with you. Often they will claim to be the spirit of a famous celebrity, or will present ridiculous ideas and expect you to accept them unquestioningly. Just say no. Remember you are the one in control, and you can choose with whom you want to associate.

Public message work

In time, as your mediumship develops, you might choose to begin to do public message work. This is such a wonderful gift to give others. It is through public message work that most people get the proof that they need to know that life goes on after death. I know that certainly was the case for me.

I find that you need to be a very self-possessed and level-headed person in order to deal with the challenges involved with public work. While the highs can be intoxicating, the lows are devastating. When you connect really well and are able to give a very evidential message that is confirmed by the recipient, it feels fantastic, and there is a tendency to start feeling very cocky and proud. On the other hand, when you stand up in front of a group of people and the recipient fails to acknowledge the spirit person (this can happen for a variety of reasons outside of your control), it can feel devastating. I can't begin to tell you how many times I have felt like crawling under the carpet, and vowed that I would never attempt public message work again when my public message work did not meet the standards that I expect of myself. So you have to have a pretty thick skin to do this work and keep doing it in spite of the occasional less-than-perfect message.

Skeptics

You can never convince anyone about the reality of mediumship, so don't even bother to try. If you are doing public message work, just give the message. The outcome is not really your responsibility. There are many people out there who are convinced that Spiritualists are either sadly delusional or are all frauds. Accept that you cannot change their opinion and do the work to the best of your ability.

Fraud

I am well aware that fraud exists, and has existed throughout the history of modern Spiritualism. Any time you have a group of grieving people who are desperate to make contact with their deceased loved ones, it is almost inevitable that other unscrupulous people will crawl out of the woodwork to take advantage of their grief. But just because fraud does happen on occasion does not mean that the real phenomena does not exist.

The purpose of this book is to teach you how to connect directly with the other side so that you are not at the mercy of anyone else.

Removing curses?

I do not believe in "curses." An honest, ethical medium will never tell you that someone has placed a curse on you, and require money from you to remove the "curse." They will never suggest that you need to buy something for protection. In fact, I strongly recommend that you strictly avoid anyone who tells you anything like this.

7

The Development Circle

Mediums can be born or made

Mediums can be born or made. What I mean by this is that some people are born with the gift of mediumship, while everyone else can develop the skill to some degree through practice. Some of the world's best mediums have been developed, while other equally good mediums were born with the gift.

I probably fall somewhere in the middle of the range. My brother says he thinks it is a gift I was born with, but I disagree. While there were events in my early years when I just "knew" something and, in retrospect, it is obvious that someone was talking to me, I can honestly say that I was never consciously aware of spirit people until I began working to develop mediumship when I was in my 40's.

I have heard people tell me that they have always been able to speak to spirit beings since their earliest childhood, and I used to envy this, partly because I had a rather lonely childhood and would have enjoyed the company, and partly because I am as lazy as the next person and would love to be able to be good at something without having to work at it. But over time I began to realize that being born with the gift already apparent is not necessarily a good thing because there is a tendency on the part of natural mediums to "stay where they start," while those who have to work to develop it can often surpass the skills of the natural medium. So don't feel bad if you didn't come by the skill naturally. As I have stated many times, everyone has some degree of sensitivity to spirit influence, therefore anyone who has the desire and the willingness to put in the work involved can become a medium.

The "home circle"

So, regardless of whether you have been aware of this ability since childhood, or if it is something that you have recently become interested in developing, one of the best ways of developing mediumistic skills is by participating in a "home circle." Home circles are often referred to as the nursery school of mediumship. The Spiritualist movement was founded on home circles.

Forming a development circle

A "circle" is a group of people who meet together on a regular basis, usually in someone's home, specifically for the purpose of learning mediumship. Basically you sit in a circle, ideally with a more experienced medium leading the group, you open with some sort of prayer, you do some sort of meditation, and sit in silence with your eyes closed, to see if you "get" anything.

A development circle is not merely a crowd of people gathered together hoping to witness spirit phenomena; rather, it is a gathering of persons who want to work together to establish a relationship with the spirit world.

It's best if you can find a group of people who can commit to attending the circle on a regular basis, but this can be difficult in our modern age. In the early days of Spiritualism there were not as many demands on people's time and people were willing to commit to sitting in the same circle for years.

The nature of society back in the mid 1800's, when the Spiritualist movement began, lent itself to small groups of friends getting together at the same time every week to "sit." It was an opportunity to socialize, and in those days before television, it was entertainment. The same small group of people would "sit" together at the same time week after week for years. Today it is hard to find people who are able to commit to getting together for even two weeks in a row. People often ask why we see so little physical mediumship now. I think the reason is that physical mediumship requires a lot more effort to develop, and most of us just don't have the time.

Ideally a development circle should be made up of not less than four persons, and not more than twelve. They used to say that it was best to have equal numbers of both men and women, but that is very difficult to do since I find that far more women are interested in developing mediumship.

Each circle should run about an hour or so, generally not more than two hours at a time because it can be physically draining and once you begin to tire the results diminish. The participants should arrive on time not only because the other sitters are waiting, but those on the spirit side are also waiting.

Does the room have to be dark? No, the room does not have to be dark. Mediumship can take place in bright sunlight, but for development circles dim light works better because it is more relaxing than bright light, but darkness is absolutely not necessary.

Some people prefer to sit on a hard chair while others prefer a softer chair (personally I will go for the softest chair in the room if I have a choice), but the important thing is to sit up as straight as it is comfortable for you without crossing your hands and legs. I have heard it said that this is to keep your energy from getting blocked, that sitting straight keeps the energy flowing freely.

I've heard it said that the "sitters" in the group should sit in the same place at each circle, unless the spirits indicate a change in position, and that you should join hands at the beginning of the circle, in order to generate the necessary energy, but I've been in development circles where seating was a free-for-all scramble for the comfy chairs and no one held hands and it didn't seem to have any impact. So if you are starting your own circle, feel free to create your own ritual. If you are joining someone else's circle then just go with the flow.

It's not a competition

In a successful development circle, there is a sense of cooperation. You are all there to improve, and the speed of your development isn't a race. It isn't a competition. You need to avoid any sense of rivalry between the participants.

I know that I tend to be as competitive as the next person (actually my husband claims that I am much more competitive than most people) and if I am not careful I soon start comparing my "performance" against that of other mediums. It's just human nature, but there is no point to it. There will always be someone who gives a clearer, "better" message than you and someone who gives a "worse" one. Besides, I can tell you from experience that if you start getting too cocky, the universe has ways of knocking you down a few notches.

The right attitude

Some people claim that you need to have a particular "sensitive" temperament to become a medium, but I think that the most important attribute is the right attitude. You have to believe that it is possible, and be willing to work with your guides.

Being happy is one of the best ways of raising your vibration, and a little lighthearted banter is great just prior to beginning the circle, but keep in mind that mediumship isn't a game, so don't get carried away with the joking. However, while mediumship isn't a game, it's important that you not take yourself too seriously either. You have to be willing to risk looking a bit foolish. What I mean by that is that sometimes you will be giving messages that make no sense to you and you will feel very silly repeating them, and other times the person receiving the message won't understand what you are telling them and you will feel like you just aren't getting it and that you are wasting your time.

The right attitude on the part of the other people in the group is very important too. Nothing hinders mediumship development more than critical or overly skeptical people. I am not saying that you have to leave aside your logic and unquestioningly accept everything that anyone in the group says that spirit told them, but everyone in the group has to understand that this is a development circle and that sometimes people will get their messages confused. So absolutely no ridicule allowed.

When someone is giving you a message, especially when it is a beginning student medium, how you respond is very important. Nothing stops a developing medium faster than the word NO. Often the medium will say something that you don't immediately recognize, and the natural tendency is to say "No, I don't know anyone like that." The student medium then begins to hesitate and doubt themselves, and the message just sort of fizzles.

Instead, if you were to respond with something like "I can't remember at the moment, please tell me more," the student medium will start getting more and more evidence and the message will become clearer. If, after the additional information, you still don't understand the message, simply say something to the effect of "Let me think about it. It will probably come to me later." or "I don't remember, but I will check with my Aunt (or whoever) who knows more about the family than I do."

Adding new people to the circle

Sometimes circles meet for a while without observing much progress. If a circle meets night after night with the same members, but without obtaining much progress, then you could consider adding one or more new members. Sometimes the addition of a new sitter changes the energy of the group just enough to dramatically change the results.

Sometimes spirits suggest changes in the seating order, or suggest other changes, and if possible these suggestions should be implemented. I have even heard of cases where they suggested that one or more of the sitters leave the group.

This is a very delicate situation. I have always heard it said that if spirit asks you to leave a circle that you should not feel hurt or offended, that there is nothing personal in the request, and no personal reflection is intended by the spirits, but I don't think it is very realistic to say not to take it personally. I know how bad I would feel if I was the one asked to leave the circle.

Eventually you need new people to practice on

After a while, the big problem with having a circle with the same people week after week is that over time you get to know all of your friends' spirit people and so it becomes difficult to prove that you are actually making a connection. For example, once you know that your friend has a sister in spirit named Alice who liked horseback riding and died of breast cancer, it is more difficult to come up with convincing evidence that you are actually talking to Alice. You are always wondering if you are just making it up based on what you already know.

My brother and I had this discussion one time, he kept wanting me to give him a reading and I said that I didn't think I could, because obviously I know all of his dead people intimately.

What could I say that would be evidence? "I've got your mother here …"

However, there have been other spontaneous times when I was able to give a message to someone close to me. That same brother and I were sitting on the beach recently and an old friend of his from high school that I did not know, and who is now in spirit, stopped by to say hello and I was able to relay his message.

One obvious solution to the problem of having new people to practice on is to add new people to your group, by inviting a few new people in. You still want to keep the original core of people, but you can periodically bring in a couple of new ones. These visitors don't have to commit to attending regularly like those wanting to develop, they just have to be interested in getting a message. I think it will surprise you just how many people there are around who would love the opportunity to get a message from the other side.

If you are fortunate enough to be able to attend a Spiritualist church, sometimes they will have opportunities for student mediums to practice. A lot of student mediums come to the Spiritualist Camp in Lily Dale, New York, every summer to practice at the outdoor services there. It is an ideal opportunity to practice because there are hundreds of people at each outdoor service. When you find that you are able to give a recognizable, evidential message to a complete stranger that you know nothing about, it is a huge boost to your confidence.

What to expect

As I have said several times before, often, when you are connecting with spirit it feels like you are making it up, so just go ahead and make something up. By doing this you are telling your internal censor to take a break, that you are just playing. It will astound you how accurate your messages can be when you give

87

yourself this freedom.

So when you first attempt to "get" something you will start to notice bits of images, sounds, smells, voices, impressions, etc. They are very vague at first, and, because they are so vague most people claim that they aren't "getting" anything, but this is not the case. Absolutely everyone "gets" something; it is just that it isn't necessarily what you are expecting to get.

I've told the following story several times in previous books, but I will mention it again here because it had such a profound impact on me:

A little while after I began studying mediumship, I was in a development class with Rev. John White in Lily Dale. He was talking about clairvoyance, and I raised my hand and said that it was hard for me because I didn't "see" the way other people do, that my messages come more like impressions, or smells, or feelings. He replied that we should never assume that we see things any differently than anyone else because we can never really know exactly what other people are experiencing. He went on to say that when we use the word "see" with regards to mediumship, we are not really talking about seeing in the physical sense, that we don't really have words to describe what it is we are doing. Initially I was irritated by his response. Obviously he didn't understand how different it was for me, but then, after I had a chance to think about it, I realized that he was right. I had always thought that when mediums talked about "seeing" something that it was like watching a television or looking at a photograph, but it isn't always exactly like that. So just because what you "get" isn't what you expected to get doesn't mean that you didn't "get" anything.

At another one of the first development classes that I took years ago, when it was my turn I stood up and said that I didn't have anything, but the teacher wouldn't accept that. So I grudgingly acknowledged that I had seen a maple leaf but that it was crumbling and decaying like a leaf on the ground in the late fall, but that I didn't have a clue what it meant.

"Who is the message for?" the teacher asked. So I just randomly pointed to one of the other women in the class, a woman that I didn't know. The woman immediately began nodding yes.

"Do you mind telling us what the message means to you?" the teacher asked the woman.

She replied that her relationship with her boyfriend was coming to an end, that it was decaying and crumbling like the leaf I had described, and that one of the main reasons was because he was a fanatical Toronto Maple Leafs fan and she resented being ignored during hockey season.

Was my message a "good" message? Well, not in the sense of giving proof of the continuity of life, I certainly didn't have a clue who the message was from, nor did I know what the message meant, but it certainly made sense to the woman I was giving the message to, so in that sense it was a "good" message.

The maple leaf in this case was a symbol, an image used to describe something much bigger. Personally I prefer to actually talk to someone in my head, as I find symbolism too difficult to interpret, and in the years since then I have clearly pointed out to my guides that I don't want symbolism if it can be avoided. If they must show me a symbol please make sure I know what the symbol means. But that is my own personal preference. Other mediums love symbolism. Over time you will discover what works best for you.

My whole point in relaying those last two stories is to try and overcome any of your preconceived notions of what to expect. It is almost never like the Hollywood image that the world has come to associate with spirit contact.

Mediumship takes time to develop

How long it takes before you start getting consistent results in your mediumship development is difficult to predict. It mainly depends on how often you practice, and how easily you and your spirit guide are able to communicate, but everyone can do it, and everyone "gets" something every time you attempt to make contact (regardless of how vague it seems).

The process of mediumship development is sometimes slow, and student mediums often become discouraged by the apparent lack of progress. I get so annoyed when I hear about celebrity mediums who give the impression that the "gift" just came to them. They forget to mention all the years that they worked at fine tuning their "gift."

Also do not compare yourself to celebrity mediums on television. What you are seeing on television is not necessarily completely spontaneous. You have no idea what went on behind the scenes, and you don't know how much footage was cut out of the final televised version. Just remember that mediumship is a natural ability that we all have to some degree.

The solitary circle

So, what if you don't have a congenial group of friends that you can get together with every week to practice? It is still possible to develop mediumship. It is very easy to begin talking to spirit people. They are around you all the time. The problem is confirming to yourself that you are actually communicating, and not simply talking to yourself. This is covered in more detail in chapter 11 - Spirit Mentors.

The world needs more mediums

Some people might disagree with me, but I think that we

have too few mediums, and the quality of the mediumship that we do have can be rather poor. Please do not misunderstand me, I am not putting down other mediums, nor am I suggesting that the quality of my mediumship is any better than anyone else, because this is not the case. In fact, I am well aware that the quality of my own mediumship fluctuates as badly as the next person. Sure, sometimes I am on top of my game and I actually dazzle myself with the quality of the communication, while other times my performance is humiliatingly bad. The key to improvement is practice, and home circles are what give us our practice.

People in spirit are not infallible

Keep in mind that the people "on the other side" that you come in contact with were human beings of all sorts; and they are not suddenly purified or made infallible simply by virtue of passing out of their bodies at death; so don't be surprised if some of the people you come in contact with have opinions that you find odd, or if they don't seem to be able to give particularly reliable information. Test the information that you get, and disconnect with any spirit beings that you don't feel comfortable with. Remember that you are in charge. You decide what messages you are willing to relay.

Censoring your messages

I have often heard it said that you shouldn't censor the message, just "give what you get." But I have to disagree. Yes, it is true that often the most seemingly insignificant thing turns out to be the most important part of the message, and you don't want to censor out something significant, but I am talking about just blurting out whatever pops into your head.

This is particularly important if you are doing public message work. For example, one time when I was giving public messages, I got a message for a young woman in the audience from her grandmother. I saw the grandmother and she was very clearly a black woman, while the granddaughter sitting in front of me was a fair skinned blonde. The challenge for me was to identify the grandmother clearly without saying anything that might be awkward for the granddaughter in such a public setting, so all I said was that she did not look anything like this particular grandmother and the young woman smiled and nodded. She knew exactly what I meant. I'm sure my evidence sounded very vague to the rest of the audience, and if my purpose had been to show off, I would have said something very different.

There are some things that you absolutely must censor:

1) Never predict someone's death. First of all you might be wrong, why upset someone for nothing. You might be right, but if it is something that no one can do anything about, then why hear about it in advance.

2) Never blame someone for anything. It just causes pain. I once actually heard a medium tell a grieving woman that she was responsible for her brother's death because she had started him drinking. It wasn't true, but the woman was so devastated that she came close to suicide herself.

3) Never predict or diagnose health problems. Unless you are a licensed medical doctor, it is illegal to diagnose health issues. Besides, just planting an idea in an impressionable person's mind is sometimes enough to make the thing happen. So be very careful how you approach it if you feel you must mention anything related to health issues.

Mediumship comes with huge responsibilities

It is one thing to speak to spirit people on your own behalf, for example, to talk to a deceased loved one, or get advice from a spirit mentor, but when you begin relaying messages for others you are taking on a huge responsibility. The primary purpose of mediumship is to prove the continuity of life; it is not a parlor game that you can use to show off at parties.

There are so many grieving people out there who are desperate for a chance to connect with their loved ones in spirit, and even if they laugh at us or claim to be skeptics, people take what mediums say very seriously, so watch what messages you relay. Ask yourself how what you are about to say will make the other person feel. Kindness should be your primary guideline.

"I've told my children that when I die, to release balloons in the sky to celebrate that I graduated. For me, death is a graduation."

Elisabeth Kubler-Ross

8

The Constraints of Mediumship

The mediumistic triangle

Spirit communication could be thought of as a triangle in which those in spirit make up one side, the medium a second side, and the sitters a third side. All three sides of the triangle are equally important for successful mediumship. If it isn't working the way you hoped, it isn't necessarily the fault of the medium.

The part played by the spirits

It seems that not every spirit has the necessary skills to enable them to communicate easily through a medium. They have many difficulties to overcome, and it is just as much a learning process for them as it is for us. They may find that they are able to communicate well through one person and not through another. They might be better at physical mediumship (such as making a table move) and unable to place thoughts into a medium's mind for mental mediumship.

The spirit world seems to work primarily through thought. You think something and it happens. If you want to go somewhere, you think it and you are there. This makes it difficult for spirits who want to connect us in the physical world because sometimes a thought is not quite enough for us.

In his book *"Mediumship,"* William Walker Atkinson describes a situation where a medium got the distinct impression that a person in spirit had something important that they wanted to say, and yet the medium found that they were unable to relay the message. Atkinson claimed that this was because the person in spirit "thought" that he had spoken, but had in fact not actually spoken. This could have been avoided if the medium had said to the person in spirit, "I can't hear you, please start again."

Spirits are still human beings

Many people are under the impression that because a spirit happens to have passed out of the physical body, they suddenly know the truth about everything, and can make no mistakes, and can even work miracles. But this is not the case; a discarnate spirit is as much a human being as we are; not any better or worse than us. All sorts of people are constantly passing over to the spirit plane, and, at least initially, they continue to be practically the same kind of person that they were on the earth plane. Therefore, it would be very unwise to unconditionally accept whatever any spirit who happens to show up has to say. Persons in the flesh should talk and reason with those out of the flesh just as we would if the latter were still on the earth plane.

As time goes on, those in spirit evolve and grow and become more aware of the mistakes that they made during their time on earth, so it is not unusual for a spirit to make contact at some point down the road to apologize for their behavior.

Domineering spirits

In a development circle both sides are experimenting and learning how to work with each other, and it is difficult at first to know just what is necessary or possible. But we should always analyze what we are hearing and refuse to be dictated to by those in spirit. Spirit communication is a three way process, a cooperative effort. You don't always have to be ready to act as a medium just because you feel spirit influence, and know that a spirit has something they want to say, or be willing to oblige friends who want a message. It is so easy to feel pressure to perform, but remember, it is perfectly acceptable to decline for any reason.

Spirits have a sense of humor

Mediumship does not require that the participants assume an attitude of solemnity. In fact, profound grief often hinders communication. I have seen grieving parents go from medium to medium and been unable to get a satisfactory message and I think this is because the pain that they were experiencing blocked the communication.

I have often heard it said that it takes time after a person dies before they are able to get a message through, but this is not always the case. Some people are able to get messages through within days of their passing. I think that a lot depends on how prepared the person was before they crossed over, and how the loved ones on this side are dealing with their grief.

My grandmother always used to say that our grief causes the person in spirit pain. I have never heard a person in spirit say that they were sorry to have crossed over. They are very happy where they are and with the pressures of existence in the physical body gone, many of them have a great sense of humor about the whole thing. The only thing that bothers them is the pain that their death causes those that they left behind.

Therefore, for best results it is important to be natural and cheerful, and not too serious. Spirits are still human, and everyone enjoys a good laugh.

The part played by the "sitters"

When we refer to the "sitters" we are referring to the people surrounding the medium. They could be the others in a development circle, the people in the audience at a public meeting, or a person sitting with the medium for a private reading. Believe it or not, they play a crucial role in the effectiveness and accuracy of the mediumship.

We expect honesty on the part of the medium, but it is also expected on the part of the sitters. If they are not going into this with honest intentions, they cannot expect successful results.

Those in spirit may be eager to communicate, but as I mentioned earlier regarding grief, they are sometimes repelled by the mental attitude of the sitters. The sitters are then left disappointed and thinking that the medium was not very good, when in fact the failure was directly traceable to them, and not the fault of the medium.

Impatience

Impatience and anxiety hinder mediumship. People who are looking at their watches and thinking, "Oh! I wish they would hurry up." or "Oh! Hurry up, don't keep us here all night," etc., disturb the atmosphere needed for message work. Those in spirit seem to have different time constraints than we do, and they can't be rushed. You need to be prepared to sit contentedly in order to see results, and then results are likely to happen quickly; whereas the more you try to hurry and the more anxious you become, the more slowly things progress.

Go in with an open mind

It is important to go into a session without any preconceived notions, other than a desire to have a good connection with spirit.

The sitter might know exactly whom it is that they want to contact, and wind up hearing from someone they weren't expecting, but it always happens for a good reason. Don't be too analytical while the session is in process. You can analyze what took place afterward when the session is over.

Sometimes you get a message from someone that the sitter doesn't want to speak to. This happens regularly, but there is usually a good reason why they are trying to get through. I remember one time in particular, I was giving a message to a woman and she kept sitting there with her arms crossed saying NO to everything I said. I told her that I had a young man in spirit named Tim who passed at age 23 in a motorcycle accident, he was a family friend, etc. on and on I went and she kept saying NO, NO, NO. I knew that I had a good connection, and the young man in spirit kept saying, "I can't believe she doesn't remember me." Finally the woman blurted out, "That is my brother's best friend, but I don't want to talk to him, he's the one who introduced my brother to drugs!" It turns out that the sitter had a lot of unresolved issues regarding that young man that needed to be addressed.

That particular event took place when I was feeling particularly cocky and I was absolutely convinced that I was right, so I kept insisting that she knew the man, but most of the time, saying NO, NO, NO, will cause the medium to doubt and the connection will end. One has to remember that mediums are very sensitive not only to those in spirit, but also to those on the earth plane, and realize how easily the projection of thoughts of distrust, suspicion, and antagonism can hinder the session.

Often people go into a session with the idea that mediums are all frauds that perform "cold readings" and they don't want to "give anything away." (I go into more detail about cold readings later in the book.) Theses sitters are afraid to speak to the medium, refuse to acknowledge a "direct hit," and as a result, the medium begins to falter, and ultimately the sitter goes away feeling that they were right and that the medium wasn't very good.

While the medium has to contend with feelings of uncertainty, the spirits have their own difficulties to contend with. The person in spirit has to ensure that they are actually getting their message across. This can be difficult when the sitter refuses to speak or acknowledge the message. It is similar to being on one end of a telephone line talking away when the person on the other end of the line is silent. The spirit trying to communicate is never sure if the message has actually gotten through to the intended recipient.

Convincing a skeptic

So we can see that the person receiving the message has an equally important part to play in the communication process. This is why it is virtually impossible to come up with a message that is good enough to convince a skeptic.

In his book *"Mediumship,"* William Walker Atkinson tells the following story that describes what happens when a skeptic comes into a circle.

"On one occasion in particular, we had a remarkable illustration of the detrimental influence of one or two sitters. It occurred at a séance at which a number of mediums were present, and, under ordinary circumstances, successful results would have been practically certain; but this was not an ordinary séance - at least, not in the opinion of one lady who apparently imagined that she had been invited to discover fraud, and that the rest of us were suspicious characters. Up to the moment of her appearance in the circle we were a happy family of sociable folk, and enjoyed a very pleasant season of conversational interchange. When, however, the said lady, accompanied by a friend, joined the company, there was a silence that could be felt. The social temperature fell rapidly - people visibly stiffened and became constrained. The two ladies appeared to feel afraid to speak lest they should say

anything that might be used by the mediums, and spoke in monosyllables. Sitting bolt upright, grim and silent, they drew up to the table, and when the phenomena began they displayed no signs of interest."

"On another occasion, when some experiments were being made by a medium, with regards to psychometry and clairvoyance, a lady expressed a desire to be the subject for delineation. After one or two efforts the medium exclaimed, "I am very sorry, but for some reason I am quite unable to get anything from you, or for you." Shortly afterward the lady in question remarked to one of the sitters, "I knew he would not be able to give me anything. That is the third medium that I have knocked out." The failure to obtain results under such impossible conditions is a proof of the genuine psychic nature of the powers of the mediums. If they were pretenders they would succeed in doing something under any circumstances and in spite of such adverse psychic conditions."

So, as you can see, the mental state of distrust and suspicion is often fatal to the demonstration of spirit phenomena. This is why people who make it their mission to "prove" that spirit communication is not real seldom experience much evidence to contradict their preconceived beliefs.

The part played by the medium

Sometimes, the spirits are present and ready to communicate, and the sitters are upbeat and sincere, but still the quality of mediumship is unsatisfying. In this case the problem lies with the medium. The most common reasons for this are: (1) Too strong a desire on the part of the medium to produce sensational results, and (2) Doubt on the part of the medium regarding the genuineness and validity of the communications, and (3) Failure on the part of the medium to properly prepare for the session.

If, as a medium, you are overly concerned with producing dazzling or sensational results, you are more likely to produce the opposite than if you go into the session with a positive, confident attitude. I have experienced this myself on more than one occasion. If I go into a session really hoping to impress someone, a teacher that I admire for example, or someone who is in a position to evaluate me, I bomb out humiliatingly. But if I go into a session relaxed because there is no pressure to perform, then the results are often dazzling. I have heard that this is because when we feel pressured or anxious, our mind is too disturbed for us to "see" clearly.

Stage fright

It might seem strange that a medium would doubt the spirit contact that they are receiving, but when you understand that if often feels like you are simply making it up, then you can understand how an honest person might feel that they are not really getting anything.

So what ends up happening is that the medium becomes panic-stricken by the thought that perhaps this is merely the result of their imagination rather than actual spirit communication and will begin to hesitate, stumble, and stammer, instead of allowing the message to flow through uninterrupted. This is particularly true when you are giving proof of spirit identity, especially when the person receiving the message does not initially recognize the person in spirit.

Clairvoyance has often been described like seeing a reflection in a pool of water. When the water is calm the reflection is clear, but when the wind whips up waves and ripples on the water, the image is distorted or can't been seen at all. Our emotions can act like the wind, whipping up the surface of the water and preventing us from seeing clearly.

The psychic telephone system

Like a telephone, the medium is just the tool. The medium does not actually "do" anything except to passively act as the channel of communication between the two planes of existence. He is always the intermediary, not the active agent on either end. The active agents are the spirits on the spirit plane, and the sitters on the earth plane. The sitters actually supply much of the actual operating power, and the spirits must do all of the communication. The medium just connects the two.

Therefore, since as a medium, you are merely the go-between, or psychic telephone system, and are not performing the actual spirit communication, you have to guard against being unduly eager to please or too distrusting of the validity of the communication. You have to let the spirits attend to their end of the line, and the sitters to the other end, remembering that the medium is just the line itself. This is easy for me to say to you in this book, but not always so easy for me to put into practice.

Preparation for mediumship

Preparation for mediumship involves relaxing and calming your mind. You cannot act as a go-between when you are focusing and stressing over problems in your day-to-day life. Anxiety is not conducive to success. The best way to put aside your anxieties and worries is through meditation and relaxation. Put on some relaxing meditation music and sit in silence for a few minutes before you begin.

Mediumship is not dangerous. Remember that you are in control, and that you attract to yourself only those entities that are compatible with you. We would not hear half so much about (so-called) "evil spirits" if more regard were paid to the necessity of preparing a calm, patient, and serene frame of mind.

Mediumship can be mentally tiring; so, don't prolong the spirit contact for more than about an hour at a time. There is a great temptation, especially when the connection is very strong, to keep on going and going. Spirit contact is exciting, like a tonic rather than a depressant; but, like all other forms of overindulgence, continuing too long tends to cause you to swing to the opposite emotional extreme, and some mediums end up suffering from depression as a result, but this is not necessary if you exercise moderation.

Investigate your spirits

I have said it over and over again that people in spirit are no better or no worse than people on the earth plane. There are all kinds, and just crossing over to the spirit side does not make someone any wiser or kinder (initially) than they were when they had a physical body. So before you follow any advice or instructions that you are given from spirit you need to evaluate just how reliable and trustworthy the spirit is. Never allow anyone, whether in or out of the body, to usurp your right to make your own decisions, or exercise any undue authority over you. You are in control.

Reasonable spirit demands

Sometimes spirits ask the medium to change their posture, or adjust the lighting, or change their diet, etc. If they make any of those sorts of requests, it is not that they are being "finicky" or demanding, rather they are simply trying to set up the ideal conditions to facilitate contact.

But if the demands seem unreasonable to you, or if you feel uncomfortable in any way, simply refuse to comply and break off contact. Remember, you are in control.

Trance Mediumship

9

Trance mediumship is an advanced form of mental mediumship. As I have explained throughout this book, mental mediumship is when those in spirit place words, thoughts, or images into the mind of the medium and the medium relays the information. In trance mediumship, the spirit uses the medium's body, mind and vocal equipment directly to relay the message without it having to be interpreted and relayed by the medium. True trance mediumship is quite rare, and really beyond the scope of this book, but I wanted to include a short chapter on it because it elicits so much confusion, mystery, and fear.

Hollywood horror stories

Forget every horror movie that you have ever seen involving demon possession. Trance mediumship, in itself, is not dangerous, but it is physically exhausting, and, as we will see shortly, witnesses to the trance state can do stupid things that can hurt the medium; so, unlike the other techniques described in this book, I don't recommend experimenting with it on your own. It is best to find an experienced teacher to help you if you decide that this is a form of mediumship that you would like to develop.

The most common misconception about trance mediumship is that the spirit entity takes over the medium's mind

105

and body and the medium has no control in the matter. But this is not the case. Going into a trance state is something that is done voluntarily. It is true that sometimes the urge to go into a trance comes at a time that you aren't expecting it, but you always remain in control and you can just say no. Obviously, you would only agree to cooperate and go into a trance if you trust your spirit guides to keep everything under control and not allow anything to be said that you would disagree with.

Sometimes the medium is aware of what is happening while in the trance state, much like an interested bystander watching someone else using their body. Other times the medium is completely unaware, as though they were asleep, or they may even find themselves busily occupied with something else, like time travel or remote viewing, while the trance session is taking place.

Protecting the trance medium

Before doing any trance work the medium must have complete trust in their spirit guides, and this trust only develops over time. Just as you wouldn't hand over the keys to your car, or access to your bank account, to a complete stranger, you shouldn't hand over control of your body to a stranger either.

Once you have complete trust in your spirit guides, the next step is to have two or more assistants with you who will control the situation in the room. These assistants are sometimes referred to as "batteries" because they contribute energy to the trance medium. These assistants should be calm and relaxed. Even if not consciously aware of what is going on, the medium will be very much influenced by the mental state of the other people in the room, so the attitude of the "batteries" is very important.

The physical welfare of the medium depends a great deal on these assistants. Part of their job involves preventing witnesses from startling the medium and drawing them out of their trance state too suddenly. Getting startled and jolted suddenly back into consciousness has been blamed for causing the death of famous Scottish trance medium Helen Duncan. In her case, police raided the séance room while she was in trance and grabbed her to arrest her, causing the ectoplasm that had been created to be reabsorbed too suddenly (more about ectoplasm in the chapter on physical phenomena). Witnesses at that séance claimed that this caused burn-like marks on Mrs. Duncan's body and she was taken to the hospital where she died a couple of weeks later. To be fair, some people claim that her death was the result of poorly controlled diabetes, but certainly the shock during that séance was a contributing factor.

When Helen Duncan was in a trance state she was unaware of what she was saying or what was going on around her. Edgar Cayce, the famous American "sleeping prophet," was another example of a trance medium who, when in trance, was totally unaware of what was going on around him. On at least one occasion observers caused him physical harm by "testing" to see if he was faking by poking him with pins, pinching him with pliers, and even ripping off a fingernail. He didn't feel the pain at the moment when it occurred, but he certainly suffered afterward when he became conscious. So, part of the role of the assistants is to protect the trance medium from any sudden shocks or from any other type of injury.

The trance state

When going into a trance, the medium often becomes very pale, and experiences a sensation of falling or of dizziness, as if they were going to faint. Similar to a hypnotic state, their breathing might become rapid and irregular; their eyes will close and they will feel that they are unable to open them. Their hands and body may twitch and jerk as if they were being subjected to a series of shocks. At this point they are usually still aware of everything that is happening, and are able to refuse to continue. If they decide to allow the spirit to use them, they will probably feel compelled to say something, and may move their lips, but often nothing comes out. Eventually, the spirit learns how to "operate" the medium's body and the medium develops the confidence to allow the spirit control. This is best done in a very controlled environment in the company of an experienced teacher with a few reliable assistants.

While in trance, the medium might become completely unconscious and unaware of what is going on, while at other times the medium is like a silent observer, aware of everything that is being said but not actively participating. Once the trance is established, the medium can open their eyes, talk, and appear totally conscious. If they are actually unconscious, when the trance is over they will be surprised regarding the amount of time that has lapsed, and surprised to learn that they were speaking, more or less coherently, about things they were not aware of. Ideally, you should set up a video camera on a tripod and record everything that takes place so that the medium can observe it afterward.

Once your spirit guide becomes adept at working with your body it is possible for them to assist others in spirit to use your body.

Direct channeling

As far as I am concerned, the most interesting form of trance mediumship is where an individual spirit takes over the physical body and the vocal mechanism of the medium in order to speak directly to someone in the room. This could be the loved one of someone in the room, or another figure that people can recognize. In this case, the medium's guides enable the spirit to use the medium's body, and the voice that comes out and the mannerisms presented are those of the loved one in spirit.

It is not uncommon for a spirit, manifesting in this way, to describe their death experience and even the movements, ways of breathing, and their "last words." In addition to this they can also describe events in their life that only they and their loved one present are aware of. Once a clear identification has taken place they will then go on to discuss current events. This can produce the most convincing evidence of the identity of the communicating spirit. It is not just the medium relaying the information, but the person in spirit actually talking directly. Who wouldn't welcome such an opportunity to speak with a loved one that has passed? I know that I certainly would love to have an opportunity to speak to my mother this way.

One surprisingly accurate portrayal of this type of mediumship occurs in the movie *"Ghost"* in the scene where Whoopie Goldberg is holding a séance in her apartment and a grieving widow gets to talk directly to her deceased husband. And yes, as this movie shows, this form of mediumship is physically draining for both the medium and the person in spirit. Actually, aside from the depiction of black figures coming to take away bad people, this movie is one of the most accurate Hollywood portrayals of mediumship.

I'm getting a little off track here, but in regards to the Hollywood depictions of mediumship, the absolute worst portrayal in recent years has to be Matt Damon's character George in *"Hereafter"* where every time he touches someone he gets disturbing images of the person's life. That is not the way mediumship works. If it was this way, it would be impossible for a medium to walk through a crowd of people. A visit to Walmart would be unbearable, and you could forget about going out to the Black Friday sales.

Getting back on topic, I have to point out that this direct channeling form of trance mediumship is rare. I have seen it done, but have never done it myself, nor have I had the opportunity to speak to one of my own loved ones this way. Let me clarify this a bit further: I have experienced going into trance, and I have performed mediumship while in the trance state, but no spirit took control of my body. It was still me acting as a go-between, but with no conscious awareness of the event as it was taking place, no internal censoring of the message, and a sensation of time distortion both during and afterward.

The sort of direct trance mediumship where a loved one in spirit actually enters the medium's body is very rare. What is far more common is trance mediumship where the medium "channels" some entity (or group of entities) claiming to be a historical figure, or an angel, or an extra-terrestrial being of some sort.

Channeling

Famous examples of this type of phenomena include Jane Roberts channeling the entity "Seth," and Esther Hicks channeling the entity "Abraham." There are numerous, lesser-known mediums that claim to channel other entities.

I must admit that I am particularly suspicious of much of the trance channeling that I have witnessed. I realize that my comments in this regard will probably offend fans of channeling, and I might end up changing my opinion at some point in the future and these words I am writing might come back to haunt me, but I have seen so many examples of people claiming to be channeling some entity, who appear to me to be just play acting. I am not saying that they are consciously pretending or that they are deliberately trying to defraud people, but sometimes it seems to me that they want to be channeling some entity and the spectators want to see a "performance" and so the medium unconsciously obliges. There seems to be an element of self-deception - or autosuggestion - and the medium's unrestrained imagination does the rest.

Things that make me suspicious

Like everyone else, I like to witness really good examples of trance channeling, but often I find myself disappointed. The biggest red flags for me are inconsistent and vague messages. A friend of mine described going to see a famous channeling medium who, claiming to channel a Native American who had died hundreds of years previously, was able to talk intelligently about satellite technology and the internet and yet referred to the microphone as a talking stick. It wasn't the fact that the spirit person was up to date on the latest technology that made her suspicious, rather that the entity didn't know what a microphone was that struck her as inconsistent.

One day I had the opportunity to be part of a small group of people having an audience with a well-known and well-regarded trance channeler. Most of the attendees were in awe of the channel, hanging on every word as though it were gospel. But it struck me that everything the "entity" had to say was very vague, talking about upcoming changes in our level of consciousness, and flattering the people in the room by telling us that we were at the forefront of this new universal consciousness. Because it was such a small group, the entity agreed to address the concerns of each person in the room individually. As I listened to what the entity had to say to the people ahead of me, I became more and more convinced that there was nothing of value being relayed. Nevertheless, I tried to keep an open mind, and decided to perform my own little experiment. In my mind I told the entity that I thought that they were "full of shit," but that I would love to believe them and if they were legitimate then I would appreciate if they would address my skepticism. (My husband would prefer that I word this differently, that I be more professional and remove the "potty mouth," but anyone who knows me knows that this is exactly what I was thinking, so I decided to overrule him and leave it in.) Needless to say, when the channeled entity addressed me there was no reference to my skepticism and instead there was just some vague reference to how my life was about to become happier (who doesn't want to hear something like that?).

As I walked out of that room at the end of the session I was so disappointed because I really like that medium as a person, and I am quite convinced that she is sincere. In this case I don't know what was going on. Perhaps she was channeling a trickster spirit, which is possible due to the entity's attempts to flatter the attendees.

Earlier in this book I described how the attitude of the witnesses could have a disruptive effect on a medium's performance, and you might be wondering if my skepticism was what caused the poor performance on the part of the channeled entity as well as that of the trance medium. I suppose it is possible, but I doubt it. I went into the session really excited about having the opportunity to witness this medium's trance work, and I had no preconceived ideas regarding it.

Trickster spirits

Trickster spirits are spirits who impersonate, and attempt to pass themselves off as individuals that they are not. That such entities exist cannot be denied, but they are neither as numerous, nor as evil, as many people believe. Rather, it is just a game to them, they are simply "playing up to" the weaknesses and flattering the vanity of anyone who will listen, and can be caught out if the sitters are observant.

Never take it for granted that the controlling spirit is who, or what, he claims to be. For instance, a spirit might claim to be a historical figure who in life was a great orator like Abraham Lincoln, but then give a talk filled with grammatical errors. In which case, it would be obvious that he was not who he claimed to be. The change that we call death does not instantly cause all spirits to reform, and just as there are imposters on the earth plane, so there are imposters on the spirit plane.

How to avoid trickster spirits

To get rid of trickster spirits simply end the séance, burn

a little smudge in the room, and consider changing some of the participants in the circle.

The thing to remember with spirits is that we tend to attract entities that are similar to us. Like attracts like. So when fraudulent spirits appear you have to ask yourself what it is about you that attracted them. Did you attract a spirit that catered to your vanity?

Identifying historical figures

Of course, when the spirit claims to be some historical figure, rather than an individual that is known to one of the sitters, it is more difficult to prove conclusively that you are actually channeling that particular individual. Go ahead and question the spirit. You will find that genuine spirits are always eager to definitely establish the truth of their identity, and will go to great lengths to do so. Analyzing the language and grammar used and the apparent intellectual capacity of the spirit are useful in testing the identity. No genuine spirit has any reason for objecting to such questions, if they are asked politely. In other words, treat the spirit as you would someone in the flesh, whose identity you are attempting to establish.

But if it is so difficult to actually verify the identity of the entity who is speaking, why bother doing trance mediumship at all? The only reason to do it is to receive accurate messages. If you can't verify the identity of the spirit entity, then can you at least verify the accuracy of the message? If you can't verify either the identity or the information, just politely end the session.

Many sincere, intelligent spirits prefer to be known by their teachings, rather than by the names they bore when on earth. If the addresses are eloquent and beautiful, and the thoughts presented are valuable, they should be accepted on their own merits, and shouldn't be considered less valuable because the speaker did not claim to be some well-known historical figure.

When it's real

When it's real, it is amazing to witness. The medium's voice, mannerisms and physiology change, and they become similar to that which the spirit possessed during their earth life. The body of the medium often appears to either shrink, or enlarge, to accommodate the physical body of the spirit. It is like the medium is morphing into a different person. The medium is then able to speak intelligently about topics that in their conscious state they know little or nothing about, such as events in the life of the person in spirit.

Trance mediumship and hypnosis

Trance mediumship can be induced through hypnosis. For example, although he wasn't initially aware of what he was doing, Edgar Cayce always used hypnosis to enter the trance state.

It has often been said that all hypnosis is self-hypnosis. What this means is that regardless of who is inducing the trance, the subject is actually the one agreeing to do it. No one can do it to you. You are always in control. You will never do or say anything that is in violation of your own code of ethics, and you can come out of it at any time.

Mediumistic auto-suggestion

In some cases hypnotism has resulted in a sort of pseudo-mediumship, or bogus mediumship, in which the speaker is not a real spirit, but is merely the result of the autosuggestion of the would-be medium.

So, how do you know if you really are channeling a particular spirit and not simply letting your imagination run wild?

The evidence is in the nature of the messages and the unusual ability displayed by you when in the trance state.

Trance and transfiguration

The word "transfiguration" means a marked change in form or appearance; a metamorphosis from one state to another. Generally, in mediumship when we refer to transfiguration we are talking about a medium going into a trance and having their appearance change to look like someone in spirit. It is as though the appearance of the person in spirit is over laid on the medium.

I witnessed one particularly exciting demonstration of transfiguration at a class in Lily Dale a number of years ago. Rev. Richard Schoeller sat in an empty cabinet (more about cabinets and ectoplasm in the chapter on physical mediumship) with two mediums as his batteries/assistants, closed the curtain, and went into trance. We all sat in silence and watched to see what would happen, and within a few minutes ectoplasm was oozing out from under the curtain. At this point the two assistants opened the curtain and we could see Rev. Schoeller sitting there. As we watched in amazement Richard's face completely changed. One spirit person after another appeared in front of us. Everyone in the room was clearly able to see each transformation, and we all called out when we recognized our loved ones. What made it particularly exciting for me was that at one point my father's face appeared. My husband and I both immediately recognized him and called out to him, and he turned and smiled directly at us before disappearing.

Trying it yourself

Unlike most of the techniques I describe in this book, I don't think that trance mediumship is something that most people should experiment with on their own, but, if after everything I have said you still want to try it, if the conditions are right, if you have your assistants ready and have developed a good relationship with your spirit guides, if your guides are interested in having you develop this form of mediumship, and you are ready and willing to enter a trance state, the first thing to do is put on some meditation music and relax in a comfortable chair. Open with a prayer to whatever you understand your higher power to be. This is not for protection as some people believe, but rather it is simply to set your intention.

Then simply say to your spirit guides something to the effect of, "Okay, spirit friend, I trust myself to you. I am willing to co-operate with you for the time being, and will yield my body and brain to your control, for you to do the best you can with, and I trust you to do your utmost for the good of everyone concerned."

Then wait and see what happens.

But remember that trance mediumship doesn't develop overnight. There are various stages of development during which the spirit and the medium learn how to work together.

10

Physical Mediumship

What is "physical mediumship?"

Today, most contact with those in spirit is through mental mediumship, but in the early days of Spiritualism physical mediumship was much more popular. Examples of physical phenomena include table tipping, trumpet mediumship, slate writing, automatic writing, and spirit materialization. Basically, physical mediumship is where those in spirit act in order to create something that everyone in the room can see or hear.

While there are plenty of cases where spirits have manifested physical phenomena without the conscious assistance of a medium, generally, physical phenomena is produced by the spirits only through the assistance of a medium, and usually only when a group of people are gathered together at a home circle.

No one is really sure how this type of mediumship works, but the most generally accepted theory, in Spiritualist circles, is that the spirits utilize the energy or "psychic force" of the medium and others in the circle. The people in the circle are the power source that is drawn upon by those in spirit.

The type of manifestations produced, like table movements, knocking sounds, materialization of objects or people, etc. are determined largely by the particular qualities of the individuals in the circle combined with the skills of the particular spirits.

The value of physical phenomena

While experiencing physical phenomena is exciting, the whole point of any type of mediumship, mental or physical, is not for entertainment, but to provide proof that life continues after death and to prove that contact with the spirit world is possible.

I am fascinated by physical phenomena, and have been devoting a lot of time and effort to studying it and developing this form of mediumship because I find it so exciting to experience something that appears to violate the laws of physics. In actual fact though, physical phenomena does not violate any natural laws. It is not "magic." There are always explanations for why something works even if we do not, as yet, know what the explanation is.

The major problem with physical mediumship, and the reason why so little emphasis is placed on it today, is that it is so easy to reproduce fraudulently, or more accurately, it is very difficult to prove that you aren't faking it. But when you are doing it yourself, with just a small group of likeminded friends and there is no money involved, there is no incentive to fake it. When you personally experience tables that move on their own, tin trumpets that rise into the air, ectoplasm that forms into shapes, sounds that come out of nowhere, objects that drop out of the air in front of you, or writing that spontaneously appears, you realize that there is so much more going on around us than we are consciously aware of, and more importantly, you begin to really understand that, under the right conditions, nothing is impossible. If inanimate objects like tables can dance around and respond intelligently to questions, what else is possible?

Is trance necessary for physical phenomena?

While it is true that some forms of physical phenomena

like transfiguration and spirit materialization seem to require the medium to go into a trance, most forms of physical phenomena do not require trance.

Is darkness necessary?

No, total darkness is not necessary for physical phenomena. One of the greatest physical mediums, D.D. Home, always refused to sit in the dark. He said that the phenomena could be produced just as well in the light.

In almost all of Home's séances there was enough light to see everything that was taking place and write notes about what was happening. Witnesses claim that Home was so anxious to ensure that everyone present was satisfied that he was not doing any of the things himself that he would often interfere with the progress and development of what was going on by insisting that some skeptic should come closer in order to satisfy for themselves that he was not manipulating anything himself.

William Walker Atkinson, who participated in numerous séances with Home for many years, said:

> *"During the whole of my knowledge of D. D. Home, extending for several years, I never once saw the slightest occurrence that would make me suspicious that he was attempting to play tricks. He was scrupulously sensitive on this point, and never felt hurt at anyone taking precautions against deception. He sometimes, in the early days of our acquaintance, used to say to me before a séance, 'Now, William, I want you to act as if I were a recognized conjurer, and was going to cheat you and play all the tricks I could. Take every precaution you can devise against me, and move about and look under the table or where else you like. Don't consider my feelings. I shall not be offended. I know that the more carefully I am tested the more convinced will everyone be that these abnormal occurrences are not of my*

own doings.' Latterly, I used jokingly to say to him, 'Let us sit round the fire and have a quiet chat, and see if our friends are here and will do anything for us. We won't have any tests or precautions.' On these occasions, when only my family were present with him, some of the most convincing phenomena took place."

While it is not necessary for the activity to take place in total darkness, bright light is not a good idea either. While it is possible for physical phenomena to take place in bright light, it has been my experience that some things are actually easier to see in dim light. For example, ectoplasm is much easier to see in dim light, so if you are hoping to see things materialize, dim light is preferable. Not total darkness, as everyone should be able to see clearly what is taking place and be able to take notes if they want, but dark enough that the contrast of the white ectoplasm is easier to see. We have two lamps with red light bulbs in our séance room and these work well for us. They give us enough light to see clearly, and yet are very relaxing. However, many people just use dim white lights. I know of another medium who, under instruction from his spirit guide, has been experimenting with the use of blue lights.

Some mediums insist on darkness at séances, not because they are trying to hide some "trick," but rather, I suspect, that it is simply because this is what they were originally taught, and sitting in a darkened room is what they are accustomed to.

What is ectoplasm?

Throughout this chapter you will see numerous references to "ectoplasm." Simply put, ectoplasm is a physical substance that is created by spirits to make various forms of physical mediumship possible.

The term "ectoplasm" was invented in the early 1900's by psychic researcher Charles Richet, who was, at the time, president of the Society for Psychical Research in the United Kingdom. He formed the term by combining the Greek word "ektos" which means "outside," and "plasma," meaning "something formed or molded" to describe this semi-transparent, white, milky, misty substance that sometimes looks like fog or smoke, and other times forms into what appears to be a more solid shape.

Ectoplasm is sometimes seen oozing from the medium's body, but most of the time it just seems to form like a fog in mid air. It is more easily seen in dim light conditions, and seems to evaporate in bright light.

No one knows exactly what ectoplasm is, or exactly how it is created, but one theory is that those in spirit generate it from the bodies of the medium and the witnesses to the séance. In other words, spirits (who have no physical bodies of their own) use small amounts of the substances that make up our bodies to create a ghost-like compound that they use to create physical manifestations.

Ectoplasm warning

Because spirits use substances from our bodies to produce the ectoplasm, physical phenomena can be physically exhausting. On occasions when I have participated in séances where ectoplasm was produced, it was exciting at the time, a real adrenaline rush, but then afterwards the tiredness set in and when I went to bed I slept like a log all night. In the early days of Spiritualism when this sort of mediumship was more popular, many mediums found that their physical health deteriorated as a result of over-doing it.

Also, as I mentioned in the chapter about trance mediumship, if the ectoplasm is oozing directly from the medium's body and you startle the medium, or end the session too abruptly, the ectoplasm can be sucked back into the medium suddenly rather than dissolving gradually, causing physical problems for the medium. This is what happened to Helen Duncan at the last séance that she participated in. So, keep this in mind if you plan to experiment with physical phenomena.

Ectoplasm and fraud

There have apparently been cases where fake ectoplasm was created by various mixtures of soap, gelatin, egg whites, starch, and cheese cloth. Some skeptics also claimed that mediums had developed the "skill" of swallowing this faux ectoplasm and regurgitating it during séances in order to trick the spectators. It is also claimed that fake mediums would stick photographs of people to the cheese-cloth to pretend they were spirits of the dead.

Researcher Harry Price claimed to have analyzed a sample of ectoplasm produced by Scottish medium Helen Duncan. He stated that it was made up of cheese cloth that she had swallowed and regurgitated. He also claimed that Mrs. Duncan was able to fake spirit materialization by stuffing yards and yards of cheesecloth into her vagina and then, during a séance she somehow managed to pull it out and form it into shapes resembling recognizable deceased loved ones, all this in spite of having been strip searched and firmly tied to a chair. Hmmm; I'd be willing to pay to see someone pull off a trick like that!

Frankly, I don't buy that explanation for numerous reasons:

1) Some of the really terrible pictures of Helen Duncan showing ridiculous looking fake "spirit manifestations" oozing out of her nose and ears were actually taken by Price himself while Mrs. Duncan was in trance. Even in those pre-photoshop days, it would have been an easy matter for someone like him to superimpose the fake cheesecloth images onto a picture of her in trance, and I don't think that as a working class WW2 era housewife in Edinburgh, Scotland that she would have had the resources to do it herself.

2) Price started off as firm believer in Mrs. Duncan's abilities until he was publicly humiliated on several occasions by one of her spirit guides who stated that Price was trying to become famous by hanging onto her coattails. I suspect that revenge for this humiliation, rather than any discovery of fraud, was the reason for his sudden change of allegiance.

3) Some of the materializations witnessed at Mrs. Duncan's séances were huge. How could anyone swallow and regurgitate that many yards of cheesecloth without choking to death?

4) How could she have formed this blob of regurgitated cheese cloth into a recognizable shape while she was tied to a chair in front of credible witnesses?

I don't even want to get started discussing the ridiculous idea that she could pull it out of her vagina…

I've got numerous other reasons why I don't believe the cheesecloth ectoplasm allegations against Helen Duncan, but let me just say that I have personally seen real ectoplasm, but have never seen any that was faked.

Table tipping

"Table tipping" is the name given to the type of home circle where spirits are able to communicate with those of us on the earth plane by making a table move. Actually, it doesn't have to be a table. I think probably any kind of wooden furniture would work. I have read reports of old time mediums who could get pianos to bounce around. I haven't seen that, but I have seen an enormous, heavy oak table that required 3 people to lift actually start to dance. However, I must point out that at that particular session probably half of the people present were very experienced mediums. Most of the time, small wooden tables seem to work best. We have a very old, small wooden table in our séance room that works very well for us.

Table tipping seems to be the easiest type of physical phenomena for most people to develop. My husband and I get together with friends regularly to connect with spirit in this manner. We do not always do it at the same time, and not always with the same group of friends, the group changes depending on who is available, and the results we experience seem to fluctuate according to who is in the group and which of their spirit loved ones show up.

NOTE: Please do not contact me asking to participate in my table tipping or trance mediumship sessions. These are just small private circles with a small group of friends. There is no money involved and I am not interested in doing it for money, or with a group of strangers. I have had some unpleasant experiences allowing strangers to participate in a physical mediumship séance, so I just don't do it. Besides, you don't need me. Anything that I can do, you can do - probably better. Just try it for yourself.

Getting started table tipping

Before a table tipping session I like to give my loved ones in spirit a bit of advance notice by just telling them (either silently to myself, or out loud) that we will be having a table tipping session at such and such a time and that they are welcome to attend if they can possibly make it. I don't know how necessary it is to do this, but it doesn't hurt to be polite.

To perform table tipping, a group of people begin by sitting on chairs in a circle around a small wooden table. We have a small séance room that can seat a maximum of about seven people. We have friends that have an even smaller séance room that is a real squeeze to fit in five people. I think you need at least three people to generate enough energy to really see things happen, but I'm sure that there are other people who would dispute this. As to the maximum number of people who can participate in a session, I don't know what the maximum would be. We attended an incredible session once where more than two dozen people were crammed in two deep around a big heavy oak table.

We choose to light the room with dim red lights. This provides plenty of light so that everyone can see clearly and yet any ectoplasm or spirit lights are also clearly visible.

Each of the sitters place their hands lightly on the top of the table, close to its edge. Some people claim that the hands of each sitter should touch those of the sitter on either side of him in order to create a link, like a battery connection, but I have never found this to be necessary. Once the table starts to take off, we are generally too busy just trying to hang on to the table as it bounces around the room to worry about whether our hands touch those of the other participants.

Keep your feet planted on the floor and away from the table legs. This is partly to avoid the appearance of manipulating the table, partly to avoiding impeding the table's movements, and partly to avoid getting your feet stomped on by the table when it starts moving.

We always open with a prayer, not for protection, simply to set our intention, and in recognition that there is a higher power that we are all connected to. During this short informal prayer we invite our loved ones to connect with us.

"Raising the vibration"

Then we start singing. Raising the vibration by singing seems to be a really important part of building up the energy for successful table tipping. Songs like "Row, Row, Row Your Boat" were very popular with the old time Spiritualists. Being happy and having fun seems to be the key to producing enough energy to move the table. We have some friends who treat table tipping very seriously, and only want to sing hymns, but our sessions with them always take longer to get started, and never seem to be quite as energetic as the sessions with the other friends who are willing to sing pretty much anything.

Some people insist that spirits require that the singing be in tune, and that if you can't hold a tune you should just hum along with the group. But I definitely have not found that to be the case. Our spirit people obviously aren't that fussy. My husband got kicked out of music class in grade 2 because the evil old nun teaching it said that he couldn't sing, and as a result he refused to sing anything for the next 40 some years until we demanded that he start singing during table tipping. He may not have a future as a singer, but he definitely helps to raise the vibration in the room. So go ahead and sing even if you think you can't carry a tune in a bucket. Sing whatever the group of you can remember the words to, and make up the words if you can't remember. We have found that some lively Beatles songs work well because most people know the words.

Believe it or not, our very bad rendition of *"Paradise by the Dashboard Light"* by Meatloaf seems to be extremely popular with some of our spirit people. That one always seems to get the table moving for us. The only problem is that half the time no one at the table can remember the words so I am considering printing out song sheets or maybe even getting a Karaoke machine.

Some early Spiritualist circles used to open by having the sitters all breathe in unison for several minutes in order to produce a state of rhythm and harmony within the circle. For table tipping we have never tried that. We usually find that when you get the right group of people together it doesn't take much to get the table bouncing, but you could try the rhythmic breathing if you are having trouble getting things started.

If you have tried singing and rhythmic breathing for more than a half hour and still absolutely nothing happens then you probably have the wrong mix of people in your circle. The only times that I have ever seen table tipping simply not work were times when there was someone in the circle who either was scared and really didn't want to be there, or when there was someone who had other serious emotional or mental health issues that we were not aware of at the time.

Signs of spirit presence

Generally, when you start singing you will start to feel a vibration in the table. You might also notice cold spots forming on the surface of the table. I took a table tipping class with Rev. Anne Gehmann, where she explained that the cold spots on the table were from ectoplasm rods that form under the table to enable it to move. Sure enough, when I stepped a few feet away and looked under the table I could see a translucent tube that looked like a clear cylinder of water had formed and appeared to be moving the table.

Sometimes people notice a sense of heaviness or weight in their hands, and an impression that the hands are being held to the table. On your arms you might feel a tingling, pricking "pins and needles" sensation, as though a current of electricity is passing along them. Sometimes you might notice a gentle cool breeze passing over you.

If the conditions are right you might even start to see little spirit lights twinkling around the room. They look a bit like fireflies. This is one of the main reasons for keeping the lights dim. Table tipping works fine in the daylight, but you would miss seeing these little lights.

Table tipping fraud

I can pretty much guarantee that when the table starts moving you will think that someone in the group is doing it. Everyone thinks this the first few times. You know that you aren't consciously moving the table so you keep a close eye on everyone else. You look under the table to see if someone is moving it with their foot or their knee, but no one is doing anything. I remember at one of the first sessions we had at a friend's house I was sure that a particular person was doing something so I kept a close watch on them. You can imagine my surprise when that person began coughing and had to leave the room to get some water and the table kept on going!

We have one friend who has attended a number of table tipping sessions with us, and during the first one I could see him looking intently at everyone's hands and feet. It was obvious that he was watching to see who it was that was making the table move. Suddenly the table stood up on end and began walking toward him on two legs and pinned him against his chair, and we all took our hands off the table and it remained standing pressing onto his lap before slowly and gently setting its four legs back down on the floor. He was convinced.

After one session that my brother attended, he asked me why we don't put a video of these sessions on Youtube. I told him that there was no point in doing that. No one watching the video would ever believe that we weren't faking it in some way. It is something that you just have to witness for yourself to believe.

However, as with anything that takes place naturally, it is possible to fake it. I have heard tales of people having hydraulic systems built into the floor or mechanisms in the legs to make the table move, but this seems like just too much trouble. Apparently, in Victorian times when everyone wore long sleeved shirts with tight cuffs, it was possible to hide a ruler under your sleeve and while your hand was firmly on the table top the end of the ruler would be under the edge of the table so that you could lift the table while keeping your hands visible. But I don't understand why anyone would go to the trouble to fake something like this when the real thing is so easy to do.

Asking questions

When table movements begin let them go on for a little while to build up strength before you start asking questions. Keep on singing and if the movements start to slow down start singing faster and the table will move faster.

But once the table is moving really well, and you can sense the presence of spirits in the room it is time to start asking questions. The first thing is to ask that they show you what a "YES" looks like. Then ask them to show you a "NO." In my experience, a yes makes the table really move, and a no makes the table stop suddenly. A maybe, or an indication that you need to rephrase the question usually results in the table vibrating a little but it is not really clear one way or the other.

Questioning the spirits

Once you have a clear agreement between you and the spirits about yes and no answers it is time to start to identify the spirit. Generally what we do is to take turns going around the table and asking questions like "Is my mother here?" Once you know who you are talking to, you can then tailor your questions appropriately. Address the spirits as if there were several present, since this is most likely the case. Be polite and friendly as though you were addressing questions to a friend in the flesh.

The biggest problem with table tipping is that you are pretty much limited to yes and no questions. It can be difficult to formulate suitable questions, and it is difficult for those in spirit to get across the message that they are trying to deliver. To compensate for these constraints some people have developed a code system where spirits make the table move, bump, or knock to get their message across. Some people call out the letters of the alphabet and wait for the table to move at the correct letter. But this is so incredibly time consuming. I prefer to just reword the question so that it can be answered with a yes or a no.

Sometimes people have questions that they feel uncomfortable asking out loud in front of the group. No problem, there is no need to ask the question out loud, it works just as well if you ask the question silently in your mind.

Demand evidence, demand proof of spirit identity

As I mentioned earlier in this book, not everyone in the spirit world is who they claim to be. Especially in table tipping there seems to be a tendency to attract "trickster" spirits, party animals who are attracted to the jovial nature of this form of communication. It is not unheard of for such mischievous spirits to attempt to pass themselves off as the relative or friends of those in the circle, so a certain degree of care and caution is necessary on the part of the sitters. Don't hesitate to ask for evidence of whom you are talking to. Ask them something that only they would know. Your loved ones will not be offended that you are asking for confirmation.

Can you trust the answers you get?

Given that not everyone in the spirit world is what they claim to be, can you trust the answers that you get while table tipping? I have discussed this topic endlessly with friends. I have come to the conclusion that where timing of events is concerned our spirit loved ones are not necessarily very accurate, and where money and real estate questions are concerned my loved one's advice is dubious, but about other topics the information that we get is accurate and can be confirmed later on. Perhaps the reason they are not very accurate about money, real estate, and timing is that these are areas that don't affect them anymore.

Initially, if the answers you are getting are apparently meaningless and disconnected, don't jump to the conclusion that it is the work of foolish spirits or flippant discarnate entities. On the contrary, remember that it is not only you who are experimenting and learning, that the spirits on the other side are also learning through trial and error, and it is probably the first time that they have tried to penetrate the veil between the two worlds this way and they probably know as little about how to do it as you do.

I am definitely not advocating using table tipping to get medical advice, but I have a friend who has a chronic health condition and she uses table tipping to have consultations with her doctor who has passed over. She does a lot of research into her condition in advance and asks the doctor in spirit detailed questions regarding treatments and drugs. I asked her once whether she really felt that the doctor's information could be trusted. Her response was that she has been to a lot of doctors on the earth plane whose advice is much less reliable than the advice she has gotten from her old doctor in spirit, and her spirit doctor is free.

I haven't had much success asking stock market or investment questions during table tipping, otherwise I would be rich, but my loved ones answers are very perceptive where family matters are concerned. So my advice is to confirm as much as possible exactly to whom you are speaking and then use your own common sense to decide if you should follow their advice. You are in charge, you decide, and you are responsible for your own decisions.

Spirit "rappings"

Back in the early days of Spiritualism, the Fox sisters

communicated with spirit through rapping noises. Sometimes when we are table tipping we also hear rapping noises. It might sound like someone is tapping on or under the table, and other times it sounds like it is coming from the walls, the ceiling, or from some location that we can't describe or locate. In our case it seems to happen when someone in spirit is very excited and has something they really want to tell us. If you hear these sorts of rapping noises ask the spirit to agree on a code such as one tap for yes, two taps for no, etc.

Ask the spirits what they would like to manifest

It's also a good idea to ask the spirits what they would like to manifest at the séance. What might start out as a simple table tipping session could turn into a trumpet session or a materialization session depending on the skills of the spirits and the sitters who are present. After the table is moving and you know which spirits are present, you can ask, "Is this a good night to try the trumpet?" If they say yes, you might be in for a very interesting session.

Trumpet mediumship

"Trumpet mediumship" does not involve the use of the musical instrument trumpet, but rather it refers to the use of a cone shaped tube (like a dunce cap), generally made of tin or aluminum. Trumpet séances were popular during the early days of Spiritualism, but are very rare today partly because very few people today are able to do it, and partly because trumpet séances in the past were often faked.

During trumpet séances the trumpet rises up into the air and moves around the room and voices can be heard coming from the trumpet. The idea is that the cone shaped instrument can magnify sounds, thereby enabling a spirit speaking in the faintest whisper to be heard by everyone present in the circle.

To use a trumpet you simply place the trumpet on a table in the center of a group of sitters. You sing or meditate and wait for the energy to build up inside the trumpet, which causes it to begin moving.

My husband and I have only recently begun experimenting with trumpet séances and so far have not seen the trumpet move around the room, but we have already experienced some very interesting phenomena. One night my husband and I (along with a few other people) were invited to another friend's house for table tipping. On an impulse I decided to bring my trumpet along. When we got there I asked the others if they would mind if we tried to get the trumpet going, so toward the end of the table tipping session we stood the smallest section of the trumpet upright on the table, which had already been energized by the table tipping. We all sat around it and focused our mental energy toward the trumpet. Within a few minutes we began, very clearly, to see ectoplasm building up and drifting out of the top of the trumpet like smoke out of a chimney. The trumpet began pulsing and rocking back and forth. We found that if we held our hands up with our palms facing the trumpet we could get it to move back and forth even more. The ectoplasm then began to form long silky strands that waved out from the top of the trumpet. One after another we began to hold our hands several inches above the trumpet and twirl the stringy lengths of ectoplasm around with our fingers, causing the trumpet to move and twirl. After we had all had a chance to manipulate the ectoplasm we sat with our palms toward the trumpet and it began to lift off the table. It managed to rise up about 3/4 of an inch before settling back down on the table. Then, within a few moments the ectoplasm dissolved and it was obvious that the session was over. There were six of us present during that session.

On another occasion we had a few people in our séance room and my trumpet was sitting in its usual spot on an antique desk that had once belonged to a very popular old medium. We were all busy with the table as it was bouncing around the room when suddenly the three sections of the trumpet collapsed into itself. We all turned to look when we heard the noise, and a large puff of ectoplasm, that looked like a cloud of smoke, shot out of the top of it. We then moved the trumpet onto the table and it wobbled around and fell over on its side and began rolling around and around on the table like it was attempting to take off. It rolled around for a bit and then stopped just as suddenly as it had started, and the session was over.

There is an old superstition that says that you should never buy your own trumpet, and that it should be given to you as a gift. I don't know that I believe that, but just in case, my husband bought my trumpet for me as a birthday gift one year. It is a replica of one of the old style Spiritualist trumpets, made of tin. They sell through the National Spiritualist Association store in Lily Dale. It has a florescent ring around it so it can be seen clearly in the dark and breaks down into three parts so that when you are learning you can use just the smallest, lightest cone.

But you don't have to buy a trumpet, and it does not have to be made of tin or aluminum; you can make your own trumpet out of heavy paper or thin card-board.

Apports

Closely associated with the subject of trumpets is the subject of "apports." These are small items that materialize and either seem to fall out of the air or materialize on a table in front of you. They can be items that were originally in another room in the house, or items that no one knows where they came from. Apports have been known to fall out of trumpets on occasion. Sometimes the apport stays, and the recipient is able to keep it as a souvenir, and other times the item disappears again after a period of time. Why this happens I have no idea.

As of yet, I have not been privileged to receive an apport,

but I do know several very credible people who have received them. In one particular case, a medium who is a very close friend of mine was waiting for a client to arrive when suddenly a large clump of ashes fell from the ceiling and dropped onto the floor in front of her. Believe me when I say that if you knew this woman you would know that there was NO WAY that this was just dirt or dust that was floating around her house and that just happened to land in front of her. She and her husband carefully picked up the ashes and examined them closely. Then they examined the ceiling and the walls to see if there could possibly be a simple explanation. It wasn't until her client arrived and the first spirit loved one came through that she understood the connection. The man had been a fire fighter who died in the line of duty! My response when she told me about it was that it was too bad he hadn't been a jeweler or a banker.

Slate writing

"Slate writing" is an old form of physical phenomena that is seldom practiced today. Unlike automatic writing or inspired writing, in slate writing the medium does not use their hands to do the writing, and, instead, the writing is done directly by spirit.

To perform slate writing, the medium takes two common slates (what we refer to as blackboards) and a small piece of chalk is placed between the two slates, and the slates are tied together with string or fastened with a large elastic. Some people even go so far as to use sealing wax on the tied string to prove that the slates have not been tampered with. The bound slates are then placed on the table in the middle of the circle. In some cases the participants in the circle place their hands on the slate, and in other cases everyone keeps their hands entirely away from it - apparently it works equally well either way. A variation of this is to put two pieces of paper between the two slates along with a small piece of pencil lead inside the bound slates. You need the type of slates (blackboards) that have a frame around them so that there is a small opening between them to allow the chalk or pencil lead to move freely.

Sometimes a written question is placed inside the slate on a small bit of paper, or one is sealed in an envelope and placed on top of the tied slates. At other times, there is no specific question and it is left up to spirit to decide what they want to write about.

The participants in the circle proceed to sing, meditate, or perform mental mediumship. Sometimes during the séance the scratching sound of the chalk or the pencil moving can be heard coming from the tied slates.

The goal is that when the slates are opened at the end of the séance, the slates will contain writing: either the answer to the question, or a general message to the circle. Sometimes the writing consists of just one or two words, while other times both of the inside surfaces of the slate will be covered with writing. There are old slates in the museum in Lily Dale, which were produced in the early days of Spiritualism and contain large amounts of writing and are written in multiple colors of chalk even though only white chalk had been provided.

Another way to do slate writing is to take a clean slate (or a piece of paper and a pencil) and place it on the floor, in the center of the circle, upside down with the chalk lying on the floor underneath it.

Slate writing fell out of popularity as a tool for mediumship because it was performed fraudulently so many times by using slight of hand to replace the original slates with slates that had been previously written on. But, as I have said before, just because something has been faked does not mean that it cannot be done legitimately. The best examples of any type of physical phenomena are usually performed in small private home circles, quietly and without publicity. I think the reason for this is that in private circles you have no one to impress (there is no paying public waiting to

136

be entertained), and everyone in the circle is already convinced of the existence of life after death so there is an absence of skeptical, negative mental attitudes which tends to interfere with the free flow of spirit energy.

I have only recently begun experimenting with slate writing by placing a prepared slate on a shelf in my séance room while I am alone meditating or during our table tipping sessions, and as yet have only received what amounts to a few chicken scratches on the chalk board. It looks like it will require quite a few more attempts before I get any serious results. I have been told by other, more experienced physical mediums that the reason I haven't had more success with the slates is that I am diluting the energy too much by trying to do too many things. I have wanted to have it all. I want the table to move, the trumpet to fly around, spirit paintings to materialize, slate writing to appear, and spirit loved ones to materialize. I have been told that I need to focus on only one form of physical phenomena in order to get better results. If that is the case then, even though I find the idea of slate writing fascinating, I think I would prefer to focus on materialization mediumship using the cabinet or perhaps trumpet mediumship and leave slate writing as an old skill for others to resurrect.

Automatic writing

Automatic writing is sometimes referred to as "writing mediumship." This is where the medium's hand and arm muscles are controlled by the spirit, and are used to write messages to those present, or to answer questions posed by those present.

The difference between automatic writing and inspired writing is that in automatic writing the medium's mind is not consciously aware of what they are writing and in inspired writing the medium is well aware of what they are writing. Inspired writing is more like taking dictation. In automatic writing the mediums hands can be writing while the medium is engaged in other activities like talking or reading. There have been cases in which both hands of the medium have been used, each hand writing a distinct and separate message, and in different styles of handwriting, without any conscious awareness of the content of the messages on the part of the medium.

If you are interested in developing this type of mediumship, and you get the sense that your spirit guides are interested in working with you this way, you can begin either on your own or in a home circle by placing a piece of paper on the table in front of you and a pencil in your hand. To prove to yourself that it is not simply you doing the writing you might want to put the pencil in your non-dominant hand.

Sometimes it happens spontaneously while participating in a circle, and you find that your hand begins to make motions as if you were trying to write, or your entire arm begins jerking, twitching and vibrating. If this happens it is a definite sign that spirit wants to work with you in this manner. If you don't want to work this way just say no, but if you do decide to go with it just get a piece of paper and a pencil and see what happens.

Initially, you will probably find that the handwriting is all over the page and not particularly readable. It can take a little time for the spirit person to learn how to manipulate your hand. I suspect that for them it is like trying to manipulate a robotic arm. If possible, try to use a large pencil with thick lead like grade one students use when they are starting to print. As your hand wanders you might find your body swaying back and forth with it. The first notes are usually difficult to make out, but this will improve over time.

Try to avoid resting your arm on the paper to limit the friction. You could roll up a small towel and place it on the table so that your arm is supported, or you could try using one of the foam or jelly wrist supports that people sometimes use with their computer keyboards. Anything that you can use to support your arm and keep it off the paper will make the writing easier.

Some people choose to write blindfolded or with a screen between their face and the hand on the page so that they can't see what they are writing as they are doing it. The reasoning behind this is to prevent your own ideas from getting mixed up with those of the communicating spirit, which just results in confusion.

The other sitters in the circle can direct questions to the medium, and the answers will be written out and signed by the spirit sending them. It is not even necessary for the questions to be stated out loud. Just ask the questions silently, one at a time, or write the questions on a little slip of paper. The spirit will read them, and then use the medium's arm to write out the answers.

In inspired writing, you write down the first word that comes to mind and then wait while other words flow into your mind as fast as you can write them down; but, you must begin to write before the complete sentence is given to you. But in true "automatic writing" the mind of the medium is not consciously affected. You can read and think about other entirely different subjects, and need take no more interest in the work than you would if it were a stranger's hand doing the writing.

Automatic writing, as with any other form of physical mediumship, is such a rush that there is a tendency to want to do too much of it. Keep in mind that it is physically demanding, and you probably should not do it more than once every couple of days.

Another thing to consider is the possibility of trickster spirits. Don't assume that the writing is valuable just because some other entity was controlling your hand. Just because they are dead does not mean that they are brilliant, or have anything really important to say. As always, test the spirit. If the writings are rational, and spiritually helpful they are worth paying attention to; but if they are odd, pretentious or flattering, they should be discarded; and, unless you can change the spirit control during subsequent attempts, you should abandon this form of mediumship and turn your attention in some other direction.

Drawing mediumship

"Drawing mediumship" is a variation of writing mediumship. In both cases the spirit moves the hand of the medium, or in the case of Brazilian Spiritist painter Maria Gertrudes Coehlo, also the feet. In some cases, the spirit operating through the hand of the medium can produce amazing drawings, watercolor sketches, and even oil or acrylic paintings, although the medium on their own is unable to produce anything more than stick figures.

I attended a demonstration by Maria Gertrudes when she was in Lily Dale a few years ago. It was an amazing experience. She channels famous artists like Joseph Turner, Van Gogh, Monet, Picasso, Renoir, and more. Maria Gertrudes is a retired lawyer who claims that on her own, when she is not in a trance state, she cannot paint very well at all.

Since I am so fascinated by physical phenomena like this I got there early and was able to get a front row seat directly in front of where she was working. I was about 5 feet away from her. Although I had a particularly good seat, everyone in the room was able to see exactly what was going on because the session was held in bright light with a video camera directed at the canvas she was working on, so that the image was projected onto a large screen above her.

The session began by her assistant turning on some fast music, and then Maria closed her eyes and went into a trance. There was a pile of clean white canvases beside her, and a few tubes of paint in front of her. The assistant held up the first blank canvas for everyone to see, and then placed it on the table in front of her. With her eyes still closed, and swaying in time to the music, she started picking up tubes of paint and squeezing them onto the canvas. Without opening her eyes she began manipulating the paint with her hands - no paint brushes - and within a few minutes the first full canvas was completed, even signed by the spirit artist. One of her assistants held it up and everyone gasped with astonishment at the beauty and the technical skill of the painting and the speed with which it had been completed. She then went on to complete about a dozen other paintings in the same manner. Each full painting took less than 5 minutes to create. Toward the end of the session she tossed a blank canvas onto the floor, squeezed some paint onto it and began to manipulate the paint with her bare feet!

Afterward, all of the paintings were sold by silent auction. Since Brazilian Spiritists refuse to use spirit activity for personal gain, all of the proceeds from the auction went to support orphanages in Brazil.

On another occasion my husband and I had the opportunity to have a private session with medium and spirit artist Rev. Joseph Shiel. During this session Joe sat down and put a large piece of paper on an easel, the he put on some meditation music, closed his eyes, opened with a prayer, and went into trance. He began a mumbled conversation with people in spirit and with his eyes still closed he picked up his pastels and began drawing.

For close to 2 hours we sat in silence as he stayed in trance and drew one face after another. It was fascinating to watch the recognizable faces of our deceased loved ones as they appeared on the page. He also drew a couple of recognizable scenes that we remembered from our childhoods. When he came out of his trance at the end of the session he elaborated more on what our loved ones had said to him. It was a great experience, and this large pastel drawing is now framed and hanging on the wall of our séance room.

Spirit precipitated paintings

"Spirit precipitated paintings" are when the painting appears spontaneously on the canvas, and the hands of the medium are not involved. I have never had the privilege of personally witnessing this phenomena taking place, but there are examples of this type of painting on display in the museum in Lily Dale and in the lobby of the Maplewood Hotel in Lily Dale.

Allan B. Campbell and Charles Shourds were mediums that lived in Lily Dale in the late 1800's to the early 1900's. They were a gay couple who went by the name "The Campbell Brothers" in an attempt to camouflage their sexual orientation. They traveled extensively demonstrating their mediumship and are best known for their elaborate spirit paintings of people's deceased loved ones, which they produced in front of witnesses.

One of the spirit precipitated paintings on display in the Maplewood lobby is a large painting of Allan Campbell's spirit guide named Azur. It was apparently created on June 15, 1898, in the séance room at the Campbell Brothers Lily Dale cottage, in a single sitting that lasted only one and a half hours.

Six prominent Spiritualists were present and they all stated that they witnessed the painting being produced. Each of the witnesses placed their hands on the blank canvas and marked some identifying marks on the back of the canvas. Then, one at a time, they took turns sitting inside the curtained off cabinet with Allan Campbell and the canvas, and watched the painting progressing. The eye witnesses all stated that the paint appeared on the canvas without anyone touching it. Every time the curtain opened for the next witness to enter the cabinet, the entire group got a glimpse of the painting in progress. They all claimed that while the light was dim there was always enough light to see everything that was going on, and at the end of the session there stood the completed life-sized painting of Azure, with the paint still wet to the touch.

Over the years many people have tried to prove that spirit precipitated paintings are nothing more than elaborate frauds. I can't state with total certainty that they aren't, but I do know that I have personally witnessed so many almost unbelievable things that when there are enough credible witnesses to something, I am inclined to take their word for it.

One way that it is claimed that fraudulent spirit paintings are produced is for the fake medium to take a completed, fully dry painting and carefully paste a piece of blank canvass over it. When alone in the cabinet, they would peel off this outside piece of canvas and expose the completed painting underneath. To give the impression that the painting was still wet they would then rub the painting over with linseed or poppy seed oil.

Another technique was to take a perfectly dry, completed painting and varnish it thoroughly. Then cover it with a layer of water and white zinc giving it the appearance of a blank canvas. The fake medium then simply wipes the canvas with a wet sponge and the painting appears. The white zinc could be sponged off in stages so that it appears to develop gradually.

For either of these techniques to be done successfully in the presence of witnesses, it would require some really gullible witnesses who really wanted to believe that what they were seeing was real. How do you peel off a piece of canvas or sponge off a painting in front of witnesses without anyone noticing anything?

This brings me to the third possible explanation that has been proposed, that the witnesses were hypnotized to believe that they saw something that they didn't actually see. How do you prove or disprove something like that? In the book *"Séances in Washington"* by Nettie Colburn (revised and edited by me), Abraham Lincoln apparently responded to the argument that people would say he was "psychologized" (hypnotized) to believe that he had witnessed a piano rising up and down off the floor in

143

time to music by suggesting that the skeptic should place their foot under the piano and see if they still felt that way afterward.

The only thing I can suggest regarding precipitated spirit paintings is that you try it for yourself and see what happens. I have been told by other, more experienced physical mediums that if I am seriously interested in developing this sort of mediumship that I should place some open cans or tubes of paint beside a blank canvas while I sit in my cabinet with a few other mediums around as witnesses and "batteries" and see what happens. I haven't tried it yet.

Before I leave this subject, there is one other thing that I would like to mention. I paint acrylic paintings and because I don't have a dedicated studio space to work in I sometimes paint in the séance room. Often when I am working on a painting I get frustrated because it isn't turning out the way I had hoped. When this happens I just wash my brushes and close up my paint and say in exasperation to my spirit loved ones "This is awful, would you please fix it for me." Then I walk away and leave it. Invariably, when I come back to it, hours or days later, the area that I was so frustrated with looks much better, often dramatically so. Am I imagining it? Is it just that after I get some time and distance from the painting that my impression of it changes? Perhaps, but it sure doesn't seem that way at the time. I've seen paint drips disappear, and fuzzy lines become sharper. I am not about to start presenting these paintings as examples of spirit precipitated paintings, because I don't think that is what they are (spirit assisted perhaps?). Besides, no one would believe it and I would definitely appear to have gone over the edge from mildly eccentric to seriously delusional.

Ouija Boards

Ouija boards, or talking boards, are simply a board or piece of paper with letters and numbers on it and some type of pointer or planchette that is used to point to the letters and numbers that make up the message.

I debated whether to include talking boards in this chapter on physical phenomena because so many scientists claim that the movement of the pointer has nothing to do with any spirit entities and instead the participants are simply moving the pointer unconsciously and the messages spelled out on the board reflect what is going on in the minds of the participants. This is known as the *"ideomotor effect."* The use of the pendulum operates on the same principle. Both pendulums and talking boards can be very useful tools for understanding our own unconscious thoughts. I suppose that this argument could also be used with regards to table tipping as well.

In my opinion, the thing that moves talking boards out of the realm of psychology into the realm of mediumship is when it becomes obvious, through the nature of the verifiable answers provided, that the answers are not simply coming directly from the mind of the "operator." It moves from the realm of mental mediumship into the realm of physical phenomena when the pointer starts to move around on its own, a state which does not happen very often.

Almost everyone I know has played around with an Ouija board at one time or another without any ill effects. As kids we scared each other with stories of ghosts and demons trying to possess unsuspecting victims, probably as a result of our exposure to Hollywood horror movies and the strict admonitions against the use of Ouija boards by most churches. But Ouija boards are not a game, and they certainly aren't for children.

Talking boards have been around in one form or another for thousands of years. But in the 1850's in England, Adolphus Theodore Wagner patented a form of talking board that he called a "psychograph" and its purpose was to study the minds of people with "nervous energy" (emotional problems). In 1861,

Allan Kardac, the founder of Spiritism, referred to talking boards as instruments with which to open communications with the spirit world.

The first "Ouija" board came out as a parlor game in the United States in 1890. When Pearl Curran used an Ouija board to begin channeling the spirit known as Patience Worth in 1913 it became quite popular as a divination tool in the United States.

Most Christian churches consider the Ouija board to be an instrument of the devil and condemn its use (of course they would also condemn just about everything else that I have discussed throughout this book).

Despite being debunked by scientists and denounced as satanic by conservative Christians, talking boards remain popular among many people and there are probably dozens of different versions available for sale. Personally I don't use a talking board very often. It's not that I am afraid of talking boards, I just find the messages to be too unreliable. But perhaps I just haven't given them a fair test.

You can use a Ouija board alone or with another person. To begin a session, simply sit down with the Ouija board on the table in front of you. Open with a short prayer, not really for protection, but to set the intention for what you want to achieve during the session. If there are two participants, both of you should hold your fingers on the planchette or pointer, and ask your question. The pointer should begin to move. If you notice your arm muscles twitching or moving that is okay; just let it go and see what happens. Make a note of the letters and numbers that the planchette lands on. If you find that you are not happy with the responses you are getting just ask for a different spirit communicator. If you are still unhappy with the messages, just fold up the board and end your session. When you are done, close with a prayer and thank everyone in spirit that participated. That is pretty much all there is to it.

My primary caution regarding Ouija board use is that people with severe emotional problems can attract to themselves some less than desirable spirit entities, or can become traumatized by their own confused thoughts, so if you are having any kind of severe emotional issues you are probably better off not participating in any kind of spirit communication.

A home made Ouija board

You don't need to buy a Ouija board. There is no magic in the tool itself. You can make your own using a large piece of heavy paper. Write the words "YES" and "NO" in the center of the page, the letters of the alphabet in a semi-circle around the bottom of the page, and the numbers 0-9 across the top of the page. Make it plain or decorate it as elaborately as you want. If you want you can take it to get it laminated, or place a piece of glass on top to protect your masterpiece and make the pointer slide more easily.

Experiment with things to use as a pointer. It has to slide easily and be big enough for two people to place their hands on it. An old trackball style of a computer mouse with the cord cut off will roll across the paper quite well. A small juice glass or a small inverted wine glass will work too, and these have the added advantage of being clear so that you can easily see what number or letter they are sitting on. A simple piece of felt like the type that you place under furniture to keep the floor from getting scratched works well because it slides across the paper easily, but just make sure it is large enough for your fingers.

Spirit materialization

"Spirit materialization" generally refers to the form of mediumship where the discarnate spirit is able to draw upon the energy of the medium, and the others present at the séance, to create ectoplasm that they use to show themselves to those in the group the way they appeared in life. For me, this is the most exciting form of physical phenomena.

Some people describe it like the spirit creates a film of ectoplasm and covers their spirit body with it so we can see them. I don't know that I would describe it exactly like that. I suspect it is more like they make a replica of themselves out of ectoplasm or project an image of themselves onto ectoplasm so that we can see them.

Generally, a cabinet is used to facilitate materialization. The main reason for the use of the cabinet is that it seems to condense and magnify the spirit energy. The medium sits in the cabinet, in the darkened room, with the curtain closed until the ectoplasm begins to build up.

As with the transfiguration work that I described earlier in the chapter on trance, I don't really recommend that people attempt to experiment with this type of mediumship on their own. But if you do decide to try this it is important that you have at least two reliable assistants to help you while in trance, and to act as batteries, lending their energy to the project.

How to make a spirit cabinet

One of the best and easiest cabinets is simply a small, curtained off alcove room, or other small room adjoining the room in which the attendees sit at the séance. A large closet with a curtain will also work very well.

One of my friends had a large Victorian house with a séance room that had a square bay window that for the last hundred years or so had been used as a cabinet. We had some absolutely amazing experiences in there. When she put that house up for sale I so wanted to buy it just for the séance room alone, but unfortunately it just didn't work out.

So, if like me, you don't have a small room or closet that you can use as a dedicated cabinet, you can build a cabinet. If you have enough space in your home to dedicate a room specifically as a séance room then the easiest way to build a cabinet is to hang a curtain rod across one corner or the room and hang a dark curtain. The area that you curtain off has to be large enough to hold the chair where the medium will sit.

This is the type of cabinet that I have in my séance room. I mounted inexpensive, round black curtain rods on the ceiling and made curtains out of inexpensive black sheets from Walmart. I made the cabinet large enough to hold a comfortable swivel reclining chair and my large gazing mirror stands in the corner. So, my cabinet serves multiple purposes. I relax in the chair to meditate, and when I am mirror gazing I close the curtains and face the mirror. When we are experimenting with materialization I just cover the mirror with a black sheet and swivel the chair around to face the room. When we are using the room for table tipping I keep the mirror covered and just pull back the curtains, leaving the space free to accommodate chairs around the table tipping table.

If you don't have a room exclusively devoted to séances then you can build a portable cabinet. I have seen homemade portable cabinets made of a thin wooden frame (1 x 3's) held together with hooks or clips, and covered with dark curtains. I have also seen a portable cabinet made of plastic drain pipes and corner fittings which was then covered with dark curtains.

It isn't necessary that all light be excluded from the cabinet. It isn't a problem if some light filters in over the top of the curtain since the lights in the main room ideally should be kept dim (not dark) in order to make it easier see anything that materializes.

Using a cabinet

To use the cabinet the medium enters it and sits down

on the chair. I find it helpful to have some soft meditation music playing. One of the assistants (batteries as I described earlier) should open the séance with a prayer (not for protection, but to set the intention and invite our spirit loved ones to participate). The medium should not be disturbed, but allowed to relax and go into a meditative or trance state.

Some people like to sing a few hymns while waiting for manifestations from the cabinet to begin, but personally I don't find this helpful. In fact, I personally find it inappropriate for Spiritualists to sit around singing Christian hymns (even if the lyrics have been modified), while waiting for spirit loved ones to materialize, but that is just my personal opinion.

One of the first signs of spirit activity around the cabinet will probably be the appearance of hazy phosphorescent lights playing in front of the curtain forming the front of the cabinet. These lights consist of small dots of light that will dance about, like fireflies. These lights will flit here and there, and will alternately appear and disappear. Whenever these lights appear you can be certain that you are experiencing spirit activity.

As the power increases, ectoplasm is produced and begins to appear in front of the curtain and seems to ooze out from around the curtain and float around in front of the cabinet, like clouds of steam or vapor. At this point, if the intention of the séance is transfiguration (described in the chapter about trance mediumship) the assistants can carefully open the cabinet currents to allow the sitters to see the medium. If the purpose of the séance is to view materialized spirit forms, you might choose to keep the curtains closed to help keep the energy condensed, and the materialized spirit forms sort of float out from around the curtain and appear to the witnesses in the room.

Sometimes these ectoplasm clouds form into vague, often incomplete impressions of the human body, often missing parts.

There is no need to be frightened by this. Sometimes perfect hands and arms materialize, not attached to a body. These hands might even float out over the circle and touch the sitters.

At first the materializations appear fuzzy and ghostlike, but can then take on more definite lines and will assume a more solid appearance that can be plainly seen and recognized by their loved ones in the room.

In some cases they materialization will actually leave the front of the curtain and float around among the sitters, touching them and talking to them just as plainly as they did when they were alive. This is my goal, to be able to visit with my mother this way, but it hasn't happened yet. I have experienced the fuzzy ghostlike materializations, but never the solid form, and never of my mother. So far I have never been able to actually touch them. I have put my hand right through them and then the manifestations have all dissolved like smoke, but we are still working on that.

As with most forms of physical phenomena, it is almost impossible to convince a skeptic that you aren't faking materialization, so don't even bother trying. If you want to develop this, do it for your own personal spiritual edification, and remember that it takes time and the right group of people to see results.

"They are not dead.
They have but passed
Beyond the mists that blind us here,
Into the new and larger life
Of that serener sphere."

John McCreery

11

Spirit Mentors

Three "secrets"

I am going to attempt to tie up everything that I have discussed throughout this book and show you some tricks that you can use right now to make your life a little easier. I am going to let you in on some "secrets" that I myself am just beginning to really understand. Well, I guess they aren't exactly secrets, since lots of people throughout history have known about them. So, maybe I'm just a bit slow in getting it, but I know that I'm not the only one. Most people I talk to, even in Spiritualist circles, are not familiar with the techniques described in this chapter.

The first two "secrets" are no longer a secret for you if you have read the rest of this book. But secret #3 is something that very few people have heard of.

The first "secret" is that the dead are still with us, and they still care about us. Death of the body does not mean that the personality and individuality of the person dies along with it. The dead are not locked into heaven or hell, or some form of limbo waiting for some future event to occur. Their bodies may be gone but the person lives on, they have simply graduated to a new level of existence. Grandma still loves you and would love to be able to give you the benefit of her wisdom and experience.

153

The second "secret" is that we can communicate with these people who have crossed over. It's true it isn't always easy, and sometimes it feels like there is a huge wall of cotton batten between us, but it is possible. The really good news is that everyone can communicate with the other side, not just a select few who have the "gift." This is great because it means that we are not at the mercy of some religious leader or medium.

The third "secret" is that we have resources available to us that we never realized were possible. We can't even begin to imagine what is available to us. Because we all can communicate with the other side we have access to all the help and information of the universe, and we can use this knowledge to fill our lives with joy and success. It's all right out there in front of us waiting for us to reach out and grab it, but most of the time we are totally oblivious to the possibilities. I have often said that I think that spirits could be doing a tap dance in front of us and most of us wouldn't notice because we are so tied up in our day-to-day lives.

Life doesn't have to be such a struggle if you take advantage of all the resources available to you. For example, do you ever wish you had a team of advisors ready to help you achieve all your goals in life, whether they are business, educational or personal? Well, you do - and they are just waiting for you to ask.

Do you ever wish that you had an advisor with experience in exactly what you are trying to achieve? Are you looking for a mentor to help you with your career, but don't know any really successful people? Well they are out there, ready and willing to help. Just ask.

Are you unclear about just what it is you really want and how to get it? Just ask.

Am I delusional? Perhaps. But why not try the exercises in this chapter and decide for yourself.

The "Invisible Counselors" technique

I would love to be able to take credit for this technique, but I didn't come up with it. Napoleon Hill wrote about it back in the 1930's and even he didn't invent it. The idea of having "spirit mentors" is ancient, but it can work as well for us today as it did for Napoleon Hill, Thomas Edison, Henry Ford, and numerous others.

In chapter 14 of some editions of the original book *"Think and Grow Rich,"* Napoleon Hill described a technique that he called the "Invisible Counselors Technique" or how to use creative imagination to develop your "sixth sense." The publishers thought that this section of the book was too strange and too controversial and removed it from subsequent editions for fear that readers might question Hill's sanity. It wasn't until much later in his life that he went on to speak and write publicly again about his experiences using this technique.

Was Napoleon Hill a Spiritualist? No, he never professed a belief in Spiritualism, nor did he publicly state that his experiences were anything other than his imagination, but this just goes to show that it isn't necessary to believe in this for it to work for you.

Napoleon Hill claimed that this technique allowed him to access the minds of people, both living and dead, as a source of ideas and inspiration. He claims to have used this technique to have meetings, in his mind, with historical figures such as Jesus, Lincoln, Darwin, Socrates, Aristotle, Plato, Homer, Newton, and Edison.

Napoleon Hill was a poor young man with big ambitions. Before he started his study of success he was not surrounded by successful people. He knew that this was a big handicap and he wasn't sure how to resolve this problem. So he decided to read the biographies of successful people that he admired and wanted to emulate.

155

He then decided on exactly what it was that he wanted to achieve. He referred to this as his "very definite purpose." He compiled a list of people, both living and dead, who had the qualities that he felt he needed to have in order to achieve his "very definite purpose."

Then, every night before he went to bed he spent some time having a board meeting, in his mind, with these people. At first it felt like he was making it up, but as time went on the "Council" meetings took on a very real quality that began to frighten him so he stopped doing it. But then he began missing the valuable advice from his mentors and took up the practice again.

Getting help from your own "Spirit Mentors"

So, how do you apply this technique to your own situation? Here are 3 simple steps:

1) First, decide exactly what you want to achieve. Have you ever heard the expression, "If you don't know where you are going, any road will take you there?" You have to pick a goal and then the direction that you need to take will become obvious. So, what is your "very definite purpose?" Once you figure out this you are half way to achieving it. Most people never complete this one step, and then wonder why they don't seem to accomplish anything. How can anyone help you if you don't know exactly what it is that you want help with?

2) Decide who you would like to have help from. Who do you wish you could talk to who could give you advice about your particular situation? Do you want family advice from your Grandma, or business advice from Andrew Carnegie, or writing suggestions from Jane Austen? Figure out who would be the absolute best person to help you with your problem.

What if you don't know who would be the best person to help you? Just ask someone for help finding the right mentor. For example, my husband was using this technique to help him with a marketing problem, specifically he wanted help writing advertising copy to promote his work, but didn't know of anyone who he could ask for help. So he asked his grandmother (who is in spirit and who has absolutely no expertise in writing advertising copy) if she could find someone to help him. She agreed and within a few moments a man popped into my husband's mind, introduced himself and offered to help. My husband spent some time talking through the problem with this man in his mind and together they wrote a great advertising letter, in less than half the time it normally would have taken. The ideas were different than what my husband would have come up with on his own.

Was the man Mike's grandmother found to help him famous? No, but how many famous advertising copywriters do you know? I can't think of any. But he was a big help.

So, does my husband call on that "spirit copywriter" every time he needs help writing ad copy? Believe it or not, no, he generally forgets and tries to struggle along on his own unless I keep reminding him that there is a resource available to him.

3) Spend time talking to that person in your mind. Spend time alone, no distractions, no television, just you and your imagination. Go ahead, make up a conversation with this person. Tell them about your situation and ask for their input. Even if you don't believe that you are really speaking to someone it doesn't matter, just ask for their advice and see what pops into your mind. You will be amazed. Be sure to thank them for their help.

Why would someone be willing to take the time to talk to a total stranger and help them with their problems? This is effectively what we are asking these spirit people (or imaginary people if you prefer) to do. I think partly they get some sense of satisfaction from helping us, and besides, we are asking them to talk about things they love to talk about. The best way I can think of to explain it is that since we are still pretty much the same sort of people after we cross over as we were when we were alive then it stands to reason that we maintain our same interests, at least for a while.

For example, I know a man in the living who is an entomologist. This guy absolutely LOVES bugs. He has spent his entire life studying bugs, his entire career has been spent studying and talking about bugs, vacations from work are spent studying bugs, evenings and weekends are spent photographing bugs. Now that he is retired he still goes into work for free so that he can continue to work with bugs! You get this man talking about bugs and he is one happy camper. So eventually when he crosses over do you think he will suddenly lose interest in bugs and take up playing a harp? I don't think so. Believe me, if he is on the other side and hears that someone wants to talk about bugs, he will be there in an instant. So basically, we are asking spirit people to talk to us about the things that interested them when they were alive, and still interest them now.

I have several "spirit mentors" that I call on for various different types of things. Can I prove that I am actually talking to a particular person? No, not really, and it doesn't really matter as long as the advice is helpful, but I have had some really amazing experiences that have pretty much convinced me.

For example, for various business related discussions one of the people I call on is Aristotle Onassis. He was a very successful businessman, and besides as a kid I was fascinated by the whole Jackie O wedding on a Greek island thing. Anyway, one time I was talking to him in my mind and he used the word "arbitrage." I didn't understand what he was talking about and I asked him to explain it, and he did, basically he said it involved buying and selling something simultaneously in different markets in order to make an immediate profit without risk, basically acting as a go-between in a business deal. Later, I actually went and looked it up, and sure enough, he was right about what it meant!

That particular conversation took place when my husband and I were driving down a road in a town that we had never been to before. We had absolutely NEVER been on that road before. My husband was driving and Ari and I were having a silent, internal conversation, in my head (believe me I know how delusional that sounds, especially when you write it down on paper).

Suddenly Ari changes the subject and says, "Do you like Greek food?"

I replied that I love Greek food.

He says, "Up here a few blocks on the right is a Greek restaurant, family owned, good food, you're gonna love it."

So I tell Mike that Aristotle Onassis told me to watch for a Greek restaurant a few blocks down on the right, and sure enough, there it was! We pulled in, and Ari was right, the food was great. Now, we go to that restaurant every time we're in that town.

Was I just making it up, just talking to myself? Perhaps, but I did learn a word that I wasn't familiar with before, and discovered a great Greek restaurant at the same time.

Napoleon Hill claims that he included people who were still living at the time such as Andrew Carnegie, Thomas Edison, and Henry Ford on his board of "Invisible Counselors." How is it possible to do that? I don't know, but I suspect that it has something to do with the elastic nature of time, but I can't prove it, nor can I explain it. Hill couldn't explain it either, and he went to visit the still living Thomas Edison to ask him what he thought and Edison gave the following enigmatic reply:

"Your dream was more a reality than you may imagine it to have been."

Personally, I haven't tried using living people because there are so many people in spirit who are willing and able to help, but go ahead and give it a try if there is someone in the living that you would like to meet.

Caveat

There is absolutely nothing dangerous about this technique. You decide whose advice you are going to seek out, and what you choose to do with that advice. My only warning to you is that once you find out how useful this technique is, there is a tendency to go to spirits for advice on every little thing. That is overdoing it. Our lives are meant to be a bit of a challenge, an adventure, sometimes we have to make a few mistakes on our own in order to learn.

Napoleon Hill's *"Think and Grow Rich"*

The following is an abridgement of Hill's writing on the subjects of the "sixth sense," and "Invisible Counselors," taken from the first edition of ***"Think and Grow Rich."*** This work is now in the public domain:

> *The sixth sense is that portion of the subconscious mind which has been referred to as the Creative Imagination. It has also been referred to as the "receiving set" through which ideas, plans, and thoughts flash into the mind. The "flashes" are sometimes called "hunches" or "inspirations."*
>
> *Understanding of the sixth sense comes only by meditation through mind development from within. The sixth sense probably is the medium of contact between the finite mind of man and Infinite Intelligence, and for this reason, it is a mixture of both the mental and the spiritual. It is believed to*

be the point at which the mind of man contacts the Universal Mind.

Through the aid of the sixth sense, you will be warned of impending dangers in time to avoid them, and notified of opportunities in time to embrace them.

There comes to your aid, and to do your bidding, with the development of the sixth sense, a "guardian angel" who will open to you at all times the door to the Temple of Wisdom.

The author is not a believer in, nor an advocate of "miracles," for the reason that he has enough knowledge of Nature to understand that Nature never deviates from her established laws. Some of her laws are so incomprehensible that they produce what appear to be "miracles." The sixth sense comes as near to being a miracle as anything I have ever experienced, and it appears so, only because I do not understand the method by which this principle is operated.

While I was passing through the age of "hero-worship" I found myself trying to imitate those whom I most admired. Moreover, I discovered that the element of faith, with which I endeavored to imitate my idols, gave me great capacity to do so quite successfully.

I have never entirely divested myself of this habit of hero-worship, although I have passed the age commonly given over to such. My experience has taught me that the next best thing to being truly great, is to emulate the great, by feeling and action, as nearly as possible.

Long before I had ever written a line for publication, or endeavored to deliver a speech in public, I followed the habit of reshaping my own character, by trying to imitate the nine men whose lives and life-works had been most impressive to me. These nine men were, Emerson, Paine, Edison, Darwin, Lincoln, Burbank, Napoleon, Ford, and Carnegie.

Every night, over a long period of years, I held an imaginary Council meeting with this group whom I called my "Invisible Counselors."

The procedure was this. Just before going to sleep at night, I would shut my eyes, and see, in my imagination, this group of men seated with me around my Council table. Here I had not only an opportunity to sit among those whom I considered to be great, but I actually dominated the group, by serving as the Chairman.

I had a very definite purpose in indulging my imagination through these nightly meetings. My purpose was to rebuild my own character so it would represent a composite of the characters of my imaginary counselors. Realizing, as I did, early in life, that I had to overcome the handicap of birth in an environment of ignorance and superstition, I deliberately assigned myself the task of voluntary rebirth through the method here described.

In these imaginary Council meetings I called on my Cabinet members for the knowledge I wished each to contribute, addressing myself to each member in audible words, as follows:

Mr. Emerson, I desire to acquire from you the marvelous understanding of Nature which distinguished your life. I ask that you make an impress upon my subconscious mind, of whatever qualities you possessed, which enabled you to understand and adapt yourself to the laws of Nature. I ask that you assist me in reaching and drawing upon whatever sources of knowledge are available to this end.

Mr. Burbank, I request that you pass on to me the knowledge which enabled you to so harmonize the laws of Nature that you caused the cactus to shed its thorns, and become an edible food. Give me access to the knowledge which enabled you to make two blades of grass grow where but one grew before, and helped you to blend the coloring of the flowers with more splendor and harmony.

Napoleon, I desire to acquire from you, by emulation, the marvelous ability you possessed to inspire men, and to arouse them to greater and more determined spirit of action. Also, to acquire the spirit of enduring faith, which enabled you to turn defeat into victory, and to surmount staggering obstacles.

Mr. Paine, I desire to acquire from you the freedom of thought and the courage and clarity with which to express convictions, which so distinguished you!

Mr. Darwin, I wish to acquire from you the marvelous patience, and ability to study cause and effect, without bias or prejudice, so exemplified by you in the field of natural science.

Mr. Lincoln, I desire to build into my own character the keen sense of justice, the untiring spirit of patience, the sense of humor, the human understanding, and the tolerance, which were your distinguishing characteristics.

Mr. Carnegie, I am already indebted to you for my choice of a life-work, which has brought me great happiness and peace of mind. I wish to acquire a thorough understanding of the principles of organized effort, which you used so effectively in the building of a great industrial enterprise.

Mr. Ford, you have been among the most helpful of the men who have supplied much of the material essential to my work. I wish to acquire your spirit of persistence, the determination, poise, and self-confidence which have enabled you to master poverty, organize, unify, and simplify human effort, so I may help others to follow in your footsteps.

Mr. Edison, I have seated you nearest to me, at my right, because of the personal cooperation you have given me, during my research into the causes of success and failure. I wish to acquire from you the marvelous spirit of faith, with which you have uncovered so many of Nature's secrets, the spirit of unremitting toil with which you have so often wrested victory from defeat.

My method of addressing the members of the imaginary Cabinet would vary, according to the traits of character in which I was, for the moment, most interested in acquiring. I studied the records of their lives with painstaking care. After some months of this nightly procedure, I was astounded by the discovery that these imaginary figures became, apparently real.

Each of these nine men developed individual characteristics, which surprised me. For example, Lincoln developed the habit of always being late, then walking around in solemn parade. When he came, he walked very slowly, with his hands clasped behind him, and once in a while, he would stop as he passed, and rest his hand, momentarily, upon my shoulder. He always wore an expression of seriousness upon his face. Rarely did I see him smile. The cares of a sundered nation made him grave.

That was not true of the others. Burbank and Paine often indulged in witty repartee which seemed, at times, to shock the other members of the cabinet. One night Paine suggested that I prepare a lecture on "The Age of Reason," and deliver it from the pulpit of a church which I formerly attended. Many around the table laughed heartily at the suggestion. Not Napoleon! He drew his mouth down at the corners and groaned so loudly that all turned and looked at him with amazement. To him the church was but a pawn of the State, not to be reformed, but to be used, as a convenient inciter to mass activity by the people.

On one occasion Burbank was late. When he came, he was excited with enthusiasm, and explained that he had been late, because of an experiment he was making, through which he hoped to be able to grow apples on any sort of tree. Paine chided him by reminding him that it was an apple which started all the trouble between man and woman. Darwin chuckled heartily as he suggested that Paine should watch out for little serpents, when he went into the forest to gather apples, as they had the habit of growing into big snakes. Emerson observed - "No serpents, no apples," and Napoleon remarked, "No apples, no state!"

Lincoln developed the habit of always being the last one to leave the table after each meeting. On one occasion, he leaned across the end of the table, his arms folded, and remained in that position for many minutes. I made no attempt to disturb him. Finally, he lifted his head slowly, got up and walked to the door, then turned around, came back, and laid his hand on my shoulder and said, "My boy, you will need much courage if you remain steadfast in carrying out your purpose in life. But remember, when difficulties overtake you, the common people have common sense. Adversity will develop it."

One evening Edison arrived ahead of all the others. He walked over and seated himself at my left, where Emerson was accustomed to sit, and said, "You are destined to witness the discovery of the secret of life. When the time comes, you will observe that life consists of great swarms of energy, or entities, each as intelligent as human beings think themselves to be. These units of life group together like hives of bees, and remain together until they disintegrate, through lack of harmony.

165

These units have differences of opinion, the same as human beings, and often fight among themselves. These meetings which you are conducting will be very helpful to you. They will bring to your rescue some of the same units of life which served the members of your Cabinet, during their lives. These units are eternal. THEY NEVER DIE! Your own thoughts and desires serve as the magnet which attracts units of life, from the great ocean of life out there. Only the friendly units are attracted - the ones which harmonize with the nature of your desires."

The other members of the Cabinet began to enter the room. Edison got up, and slowly walked around to his own seat. Edison was still living when this happened. It impressed me so greatly that I went to see him, and told him about the experience. He smiled broadly, and said, "Your dream was more a reality than you may imagine it to have been." He added no further explanation to his statement.

These meetings became so realistic that I became fearful of their consequences, and discontinued them for several months. The experiences were so uncanny, I was afraid if I continued them I would lose sight of the fact that the meetings were purely experiences of my imagination.

Some six months after I had discontinued the practice I was awakened one night, or thought I was, when I saw Lincoln standing at my bedside. He said, "The world will soon need your services. It is about to undergo a period of chaos which will cause men and women to lose faith, and become panic stricken. Go ahead with your work and complete your philosophy. That is your mission in life. If you neglect it, for any cause whatsoever, you will be reduced to a primal state, and be compelled to retrace the cycles through which you have passed during thousands of years.

I was unable to tell, the following morning, whether I had dreamed this, or had actually been awake, and I have never since found out which it was, but I do know that the dream, if it were a dream, was so vivid in my mind the next day that I resumed my meetings the following night.

At our next meeting, the members of my Cabinet all filed into the room together, and stood at their accustomed places at the Council Table, while Lincoln raised a glass and said, "Gentlemen, let us drink a toast to a friend who has returned to the fold."

After that, I began to add new members to my Cabinet, until now it consists of more than fifty, among them Christ, St. Paul, Galileo, Copernicus, Aristotle, Plato, Socrates, Homer, Voltaire, Bruno, Spinoza, Drummond, Kant, Schopenhauer, Newton, Confucius, Elbert Hubbard, Brann, Ingersol, Wilson, and William James.

This is the first time that I have had the courage to mention this. Heretofore, I have remained quiet on the subject, because I knew, from my own attitude in connection with such matters, that I would be misunderstood if I described my unusual experience. I have been emboldened now to reduce my experience to the printed page, because I am now less concerned about what "they say" than I was in the years that have passed. One of the blessings of maturity is that it sometimes brings one greater courage to be truthful, regardless of what those who do not understand, may think or say.

Lest I be misunderstood, I wish here to state most emphatically, that I still regard my Cabinet meetings as being purely imaginary, but I feel entitled to suggest that, while the members of my Cabinet may be purely fictional, and the meetings existent only in my own imagination, they have led me into glorious paths of adventure, rekindled an appreciation of true greatness, encouraged creative endeavor, and emboldened the expression of honest thought.

Somewhere in the cell-structure of the brain, is located an organ which receives vibrations of thought ordinarily called "hunches." So far, science has not discovered where this organ of the sixth sense is located, but this is not important. The fact remains that human beings do receive accurate knowledge, through sources other than the physical senses. Such knowledge, generally, is received when the mind is under the influence of extraordinary stimulation. Any emergency which arouses the emotions, and causes the heart to beat more rapidly than normal may, and generally does, bring the sixth sense into action. Anyone who has experienced a near accident while driving, knows that on such occasions, the sixth sense often comes to one's rescue, and aids, by split seconds, in avoiding the accident.

These facts are mentioned preliminary to a statement of fact which I shall now make, namely, that during my meetings with the "Invisible Counselors" I find my mind most receptive to ideas, thoughts, and knowledge which reach me through the sixth sense. I can truthfully say that I owe entirely to my "Invisible Counselors" full credit for such ideas, facts, or knowledge as I received through "inspiration."

On scores of occasions, when I have faced emergencies, some of them so grave that my life was in jeopardy, I have been miraculously guided past these difficulties through the influence of my "Invisible Counselors."

My original purpose in conducting Council meetings with imaginary beings, was solely that of impressing my own subconscious mind, through the principle of auto-suggestion, with certain characteristics which I desired to acquire. In more recent years, my experimentation has taken on an entirely different trend. I now go to my imaginary counselors with every difficult problem which confronts me and my clients. The results are often astonishing, although I do not depend entirely on this form of Counsel.

You, of course, have recognized that this chapter covers a subject with which a majority of people are not familiar. The sixth sense is a subject that will be of great interest and benefit to the person whose aim is to accumulate vast wealth, but it need not claim the attention of those whose desires are more modest.

Henry Ford, undoubtedly understands and makes practical use of the sixth sense. His vast business and financial operations make it necessary for him to understand and use this principle. The late Thomas A. Edison understood and used the sixth sense in connection with the development of inventions, especially those involving basic patents, in connection with which he had no human experience and no accumulated knowledge to guide him, as was the case while he was working on the talking machine, and the moving picture machine.

Nearly all great leaders, such as Napoleon, Bismark, Joan of Arc, Christ, Buddha, Confucius, and Mohammed, understood, and probably made use of the sixth sense almost continuously. The major portion of their greatness consisted of their knowledge of this principle.

"Tricks and treachery are the practice of fools, that don't have brains enough to be honest."

Benjamin Franklin

12

Fraud

The whole purpose of this book is to enable the reader to connect with spirit directly, so that you are not dependent on visits to mediums to make contact with your loved ones or spirit mentors. I'm not saying that you should never have a reading with a medium. We all love to get a reading from someone else that proves to us the continuity of life after death. I know that I certainly do. However, any time you have a group of people who are grieving and who are willing to pay, often large sums of money, for one more chance to speak to a loved one, there will always be con artists looking for a way to take advantage of them.

I am not suggesting that most mediums are frauds. In fact, over the years I have gotten to know lots of mediums and, with very few exceptions, I have found them to be honest, sincere people who work very hard to help people who are grieving. If you are in it for the money, let me tell you that there are a lot of easier ways to make a buck. I have included this chapter on fraud, not to teach you how to take advantage of people, but to show you some of the tricks that fake mediums use to make it appear they are making contact with spirit.

Basically, there are two types of tricks that people use to fake mental mediumship: 1) hot readings, and 2) cold readings.

Hot reading

Hot reading is where the fake medium does research in advance to find out information about the client and their deceased loved ones that they then pretend to hear directly from spirit. This is the kind of fraud that most people think of when they get a really good message. They think, "How did she know that? Someone must have told her, she must have done some research before I got here."

Frankly, this is the least likely form of deception that you are ever going to run into. Sure, I have occasionally heard some unsubstantiated reports of fraudulent mediums who had microphones set up in waiting rooms, and assistants that would chat with the client in advance and relay the information to the medium prior to the session, but realistically the amount of money involved does not usually justify going to this much trouble.

I have heard reports - but I have no idea if they are accurate - of television shows where the medium has people planted in the line-ups waiting to get in, who would then start up conversations to get information that the reader can use in their "performance." If this does happen I suspect it is because the medium is afraid that, for whatever reason, when they get up to "perform" that they won't be able to do it, and this is a form of insurance for them. I don't condone the practice, but I can see why someone would do it.

Also, regarding television mediumship, you have to realize that the finished product that you see on TV is not exactly what those in the studio audience witnessed. The production company always ends up cutting and editing to make it look more impressive, so don't compare the average medium giving public demonstrations for free in a Spiritualist church with a celebrity medium getting paid thousands of dollars on a television show.

Cold reading

Cold reading basically involves using techniques that get the subject to reveal information about them self while making it appear that the information is coming from the reader. This is done through reading body language, and through the deliberate use of statements (often referred to as "Barnum statements" after the American showman P.T. Barnum), that seem personal, yet can apply to almost anybody. This technique is based on "the Forer effect" which was named after psychologist Bertram R. Forer, who designed a study in 1948 which showed that people tend to give high accuracy ratings to descriptions of their personality that they believe to be specific to them (such as personality tests or psychic readings), but which are in fact vague and general enough to apply to anyone.

In cold readings, these statements are used to elicit identifying/positive responses from the subject. The statements can then be expanded into longer and more elaborate statements that appear to reveal large amounts of detail about the subject.

Examples of Barnum/Forer statements include:

"You sometimes feel insecure, especially around strangers."

"You have old photographs that you haven't looked at in some time."

"There are aspects of your job that you don't enjoy."

"There is someone in your life that you are having problems with."

"Your grandmother passed over as a result of issues in her chest or abdomen."

We can all identify with these statements. Regarding the last statement, the vast majority of deaths result from issues involving the chest or abdomen, in fact, I think I can safely say that absolutely everyone's heart stops beating at the time of death.

These "Barnum statements" work because people are so eager to make a connection between what the reader is saying and some aspect of their own lives that they will search their memory and reinterpret the statement in a variety of possible ways in order to make it apply.

The rainbow ruse

The "rainbow ruse" is similar to Barnum statements, but in this case, the "psychic" makes a general statement about a personality trait that the subject has, but then covers all the possibilities by also attributing the opposite trait to the subject. Basically, they take a common personality trait, then the opposite of that trait and combine the two together in a statement.

Examples of rainbow ruse statements include:

> *"You are generally a very patient and understanding person, but in some situations, you can be impatient."*

> *"You try to be careful with your money, but there are times when you like to splurge."*

> *"You are a very kind and considerate person, but there have been times when you have behaved in unkind ways that you aren't proud of."*

> *"You are popular and can be the life of the party, but sometimes you prefer to stay more in the background."*

Although these statements are contradictory, the technique

works because everyone exhibits these types of contradictions in their personalities.

A cold reading requires the subject's participation. One way the cold reader elicits this participation from the subject is by saying something such as:

> *"Sometimes the images they show can mean more to you than to me; so if I am misinterpreting something please point it out to me so I can do a better job of relaying the information from your loved ones in the spirit world."*

Everyone, including the most skeptical of subjects, would truly love to get a message from a loved one in spirit, so it is only natural, if the reader is likeable and manages to inspire confidence in the subject, that the subject would be inclined to reinterpret vague statements in such a way that will make it appear that the reader is making specific statements or predictions.

The reader begins by making a number of vague statements (these can also be framed as questions), and the subject then reveals further information through their replies (whether verbal or non-verbal). The cold reader then focuses on the positive responses from the subject and drops the topics that didn't "hit." In this way, the reader appears to be making startling revelations, but the information is actually coming from the subject, and is then restated by the reader, which then reinforces the idea that the reader got something correct. So while the reader does most of the talking, it is actually the subject who provides the information.

Reading body language

Subtle cues such as changes in facial expression can indicate whether a particular topic is a hit or a miss. The cold reader carefully observes the subject's reactions and then refines the original statements according to the subject's body language.

Shotgunning

"Shotgunning" is a technique that is sometimes used in public demonstrations of mediumship. In Spiritualist circles it is called giving "spirit centered" versus "client centered" readings. This is where the medium makes one or more broad general statements, such as "Who can take the name Bill or William?" Half the hands in the audience shoot up, so the medium narrows down the number of raised hands by making additional statements such as "He has a father or grandfather type energy, and liked to spend time outdoors."

When you see a medium doing a public demonstration of this type of "spirit centered" mediumship it does NOT necessarily mean that they are frauds who are doing cold readings. I often do this form of message work, and it is very commonly performed in Britain. I like to use this style when I have a very clear spirit communicator but I am not initially totally sure whom the message is for. Also, sometimes you get two or three people in spirit with the same identifying information who want to send messages to their loved ones in the audience and so they "piggyback" their messages in order to save time.

The difference between a legitimate medium who is doing "spirit centered" mediumship and someone doing a cold reading is that as the cold reader makes these statements they watch the audience for reactions, and choose someone whose body language makes them appear to be cooperative and eager to get a message. They then "go fishing" by asking vague questions from their cooperative subject in such a way that they can be perceived as statements. The goal is to get as many "yes" responses as possible from the subject which causes the subject to believe that they are connecting with spirit, and also allowing the medium to impress the entire audience.

Public message work usually ends with a specific message

from the spirit loved one, and cold readers basically tell the subject what they want to hear, which is usually a very vague message that everything will turn out well.

Unconscious cold reading

It is possible for sincere mediums who have never intended to defraud anyone to fall into the trap of using unconscious cold reading techniques such as "shotgunning" because it can be easier and less intimidating to make vague statements to suit a cooperative subject than to focus exclusively on the spirit. The best way to ensure that you are not doing this is to make sure that you are speaking directly to a particular spirit and don't fall into the trap of making your statements too vague. When I know that I am speaking to someone in spirit I demand that they give me very specific, unique information, no "grandmothers baking cookies." I want details that are so specific that no one can accuse me of being vague.

Everybody has an interesting and unique story to tell, and when they give me very specific information about their lives I know without a doubt that the information is accurate because I know that I couldn't possibly make most of this stuff up. For example, one time when I was doing a public message service I got a husband and wife in spirit who had a very volatile relationship and wanted to get a message to their daughter who was in the audience. That is pretty vague, so I demanded more information. They told me that the wife crossed over first, and then the husband. Still too vague. Then they talked about their very ugly divorce. Not good enough, I mean really, what divorce isn't ugly? Finally they told me about a fight they had where the wife stabbed the husband with a barbecue fork. Believe me, the daughter knew exactly what they were talking about!

The best way to ensure that you are not unconsciously doing a cold reading is to not ask questions. I have a bit of an advantage when doing public message work because I am a bit near sighted and can't really see anyone beyond the first few rows and my hearing is impaired and I can't really hear their responses too clearly anyway, so I find it much easier to just talk to spirit.

Also, since the vast majority of people who come to see a medium or a psychic for a private reading come for advice regarding the same few issues (ie. money, family, love, work), it is easy to begin to guess why the person is there, and start the session by making comments about one of these common concerns and see where the client takes the reading from there. So try to clear your mind and try not to make assumptions about people.

Profiling or making assumptions about the subject

A skilled cold reader carefully observes the subject while looking for visible clues about them and makes assumptions based on what they observe. Their age, the way they dress, and the presence of a wedding ring are just a few of the clues that are used to make assumptions about the subject and thus begin the statement/questioning process.

Some common cold reader statements include: "You are struggling to make a decision." or "There are big changes happening in your life." Duh, who isn't experiencing some sort of change in their life, and who doesn't have a decision to make, even if it is just about where to go for lunch. But since the subject really wants to believe that the reader is legitimate they will assume that the reader actually knows about their situation and will volunteer even more information.

"Claiming" the subject's answers

A lot of what a cold reader does involves simply repeating back what the subject has said. If the cold reader does this skillfully enough it appears that they already knew the answer and the subject will tend to forget that they that gave the cold reader the information in the first place.

Suppose the subject confirms that they have a decision to make. The reader can simply say, "Yes, that's right," thereby "claiming" the answer. The more information that the reader "claims" the more convinced the subject becomes that the reader knew the information.

The strategic use of pauses

One very successful method of fishing for information is the strategic use of silence. For example, the reader might say, "You are struggling to make a decision." and then pause long enough for the subject to elaborate about the decision. Even if the subject doesn't respond, their body language will show whether or not the reader is on the right track.

Contact with the spirit world is real; you don't need tricks to do it

As I pointed out at the beginning of this chapter, most mediums are sincere and ethical individuals who are not in it for the money. So even though it is possible to use tricks and techniques like the ones I have described here, it really isn't necessary. Spirit contact is real. The big advantage of learning how to develop your own connection with those in spirit is that you will know beyond a shadow of a doubt that spirit communication is real.

Imagine how different our world would be if everyone realized that life is eternal and that our loved ones are not burning in some sort of eternal hell. We need more mediums, so I sincerely hope you will use the information in this book to try it for yourself.

Irene McGarvie

Index

Other books by Irene McGarvie

The Sweat Lodge is for Everyone

The Native American Sweat Lodge Ceremony offers so many benefits, both spiritual and physical for anyone who has the opportunity to take part in one.

This book is the non-Native's guide to understanding, participating in, and benefiting from Native American Sweat Lodge ceremonies. Learn how to incorporate Native American religious beliefs into your own Spiritual practice and get in touch with Mother Earth's energy.

Pious Fraud

This book shows how all of our present day western religious beliefs came from one early form of religion, and how religious leaders throughout history have adapted these religious beliefs in an attempt to control their followers.

As you read this book you will discover that the literal "truths" and "historical events" that are espoused by our churches, and have formed much of our present day religious beliefs, were actually based on much earlier pagan myths, particularly that of Solar Worship or Astrolatry.

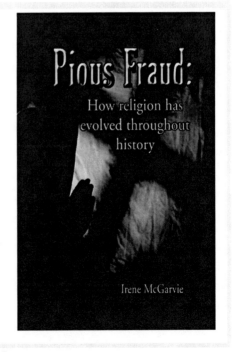

Other books by Irene McGarvie

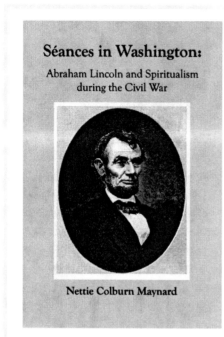

Séances in Washington:
Abraham Lincoln and Spiritualism
during the Civil War

Nettie Colburn Maynard

Séances in Washington

This book is the first-hand account of the experiences of a Spiritualist medium in Washington during the Civil War. Spiritualism was at its peak of popularity. Nettie Colburn was a young woman from a modest family who through her gift of trance mediumship found herself mingling with the elite of Washington society, and ultimately helping to influence the course of U.S. history.

This book was originally published in 1891 under the title *"Was Abraham Lincoln a Spiritualist?"* This book has been revised and edited by Spiritualist minister Irene McGarvie.

The Spirituality of Money

Most people have false beliefs about money. Our religions subtly tell us that having money is evil. The media tells us that times are tough and money is scarce. But beliefs like these prevent us from enjoying the life of affluence and abundance that we deserve.

Find out what the Bible really has to say about money.

This book will help you to examine your beliefs about money and change the patterns that have been holding you back.

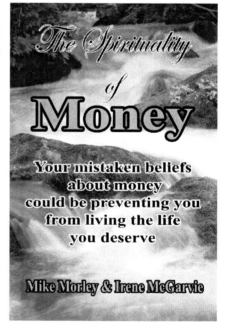

The Spirituality of Money

Your mistaken beliefs about money could be preventing you from living the life you deserve

Mike Morley & Irene McGarvie

Other books by Irene McGarvie

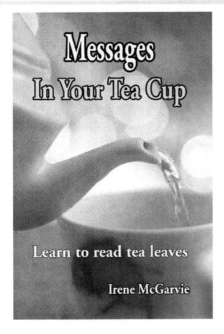

Messages in your Tea Cup

Have you ever wished that you could predict the future?

Throughout history people all over the world have been able to predict future events and get advice from "beyond" through tea leaf reading. It was popular because it worked so well and the necessary materials could be found in any kitchen.

Tea leaf reading is something that anyone can do. Messages in Your Tea Cup will teach you everything you need to know to begin reading tea leaves immediately.

Have You Lived Before?

Have you ever had the feeling that you have lived before? Most religions throughout history have held a belief in reincarnation. Even the early Christians believed it. Is it possible?

Find out what many of the great thinkers throughout history believed and decide for yourself.

This book is an updated version of *"Reincarnation and the Law of Karma"* written by William Walker Atkinson and originally published in 1908. This revised version has been edited by Spiritualist minister Irene McGarvie.

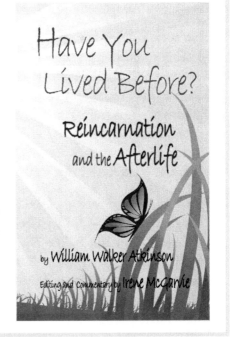

Other books by Irene McGarvie

Mirror Gazing

Many people who have experienced Mirror Gazing consider it to be a technique which allows you to see and interact with the spirits of departed loved ones. Great inventors throughout history have used it as a means of tapping into their creative abilities.

For centuries churches have condemned mirror gazing as satanic or evil, and yet many Biblical figures used a form of it to receive Divine guidance.

So which is it, a useful skill or a demonic tool? Read this book and decide for yourself

Change Your Thoughts, Change Your Life

This book explains how our thoughts affect our emotions and ultimately determine our success in life. It shows how we can be influenced by the thoughts of others around us, even if we don't realize that it's happening, and how we can choose to manage our thoughts in order to create the life that we desire.

This is an updated version of the New Thought classic *"Thought Vibration; Or the Law of Attraction in the Thought World,"* written by William Walker Atkinson, and originally published in 1906, revised and updated by Spiritualist minister Irene McGarvie.

Change Your Thoughts, Change Your Life!

Using the power of your mind to create your ideal life

William Walker Atkinson
Editing & Commentary by Irene McGarvie

Other books by Irene McGarvie

The Future is in Your Hands

Palm Reading Made Easy. A face might wear a mask, but hands don't lie! Future events and past influences are all marked out on our hands, there for anyone with the knowledge to see. This book teaches how to predict the future and understand yourself and others through studying the shape of the hand and fingers.

This book was originally published in 1916. The original work has been totally revised and updated by Spiritualist minister and author Irene McGarvie to make it easier for modern day readers to understand.

About the author:

Rev. Irene McGarvie is an ordained Spiritualist Minister with the Spiritualist Church of Canada, and the City of Light Spiritualist Church in New York State.

Irene enjoys exploring all aspects of mediumship and psychic development. She has written and co-written numerous books on spirituality, divination, and spiritual development.

To learn more about the author visit:
www.irenemcgarvie.com

To discover more books about
personal development, spirituality
and divination visit:

www.learnancientwisdom.com

CPSIA information can be obtained at www.ICGtesting.com
Printed in the USA
BVOW040048050612

291696BV00004B/2/P